MY LIFE
in the
WAITING ROOMS

MY LIFE
in the
WAITING ROOMS

A Saga about My Health Issues:
Cancer and a Mystery Disease

JOHN F. WELSH JR.

MY LIFE IN THE WAITING ROOMS
A Saga about My Health Issues: Cancer and a Mystery Disease

iUniverse books may be ordered through booksellers or by contacting:

iUniverse
1663 Liberty Drive
Bloomington, IN 47403
www.iuniverse.com
1-800-Authors (1-800-288-4677)

Because of the dynamic nature of the Internet, any web addresses or links contained in this book may have changed since publication and may no longer be valid. The views expressed in this work are solely those of the author and do not necessarily reflect the views of the publisher, and the publisher hereby disclaims any responsibility for them.

Any people depicted in stock imagery provided by Thinkstock are models, and such images are being used for illustrative purposes only. Certain stock imagery © Thinkstock.

ISBN: 978-1-4917-7452-6 (sc)
ISBN: 978-1-4917-7453-3 (e)

Library of Congress Control Number: 2015913045

Print information available on the last page.

iUniverse rev. date: 09/17/2015

This Book Is Dedicated to
My Doctors and Special People:

Dr. Kevin Bright

Ear, Nose, Throat Specialist
Southwest ENT Consultants

Dr. Aime Serna

Internal Medicine
El Paso Internists PA

Dr. Panagoitis Valilis

Oncologist-Chemotherapy
Texas Oncology

Dr. Humberto Serna

Nephrologist
El Paso Kidney Specialists

Dr. Ben Matthew

Cardiologist
El Paso Heart Center

Dr. Adrian Guevara

Dermatologist
Sun City Dermatology

_____ and: _____

Nancy Silva

Spinal & Rehab
Specialists

Jennifer Armendariz

Texas Oncology
With Doctor Valilis

Ruth Sullivan

Texas Oncology
With Doctor Valilis

CONTENTS

PREFACE

WHEN I GOT SERIOUS about writing this book in late 2012, I knew that a few thousand words would not make the *New York Times* best-sellers list. I did not think about it being published or made to look like a real book---like something *very* important. What I did think about was putting down in journal-form my experiences with doctors and the manner in which they handled my health issues which---at that time--- involved only cancer and its treatment.

But then, as my health issues changed and became worse, I thought it would be a good idea to include the changes and the serious effects I was stuck with. And, like some ambitious author, I thought this book would be very helpful to senior citizens like myself, and to those families who have elderly members trying to enjoy their later years.

So, that's what this book is about. In a nutshell, it takes me from an initial series of appointments with different doctors though diagnosis, preparation for treatment, treatment, and my remission---hopefully a full recovery---from cancer through another series of appointments with other---but sometimes the same---doctors through diagnosis, preparation for treatment, treatment, and the aftermath---where I am today---from Bell's Palsy.

You probably know very little about Bell's Palsy. I call it a "mystery disease," because that's what I found it to be. It prompted several surgeries, completely changed the way I look, and---to a degree---how I feel.

Take this book for what it is: a primer to help you through health issues that you might incur as you move through your senior years.

One final suggestion: enjoy those hours you will spend in the waiting rooms as you ... well, wait and wait a little longer.

INTRODUCTION

SINCE SEPTEMBER 2012, I have spent hundreds of hours---maybe more---in various waiting rooms in doctors' offices, hospitals, out-patient clinics, in-patient clinics, and rehab centers. And, in just about all cases, my wife, Mary, has been sitting next to me. Both of us waiting.

During this 30-plus month period of time, I have become a self-appointed expert on waiting rooms. Here is what I have observed (in no special order):

- All chairs in all waiting rooms come from the same factory. It is owned by doctors.
- The vinyl or cloth upholstery will not last very long. It is usually stained anyway.
- The vinyl or cloth upholstery is usually too flowery.
- It matches nothing, except maybe the floor tile or the Formica counter top.
- The padding under the upholstery is not comfortable. Styrofoam would be better.
- The wooden arms on the chairs scratch easily.
- The matching tables usually don't match the chairs. Not even each other.
- The aisles between rows of chairs are too narrow.
- Patients in most waiting rooms are overwhelmingly new mothers.
- The baby carriages---or whatever they're called today---are huge.
- Some carriages are about the same size as a Volkswagen beetle.

- Most baby carriages are loaded with enough blankets to heat up Antarctica.
- Most babies in the carriages cry a lot.
- Most babies not in the carriages cry a lot.
- Most of the mothers want to cry a lot.
- The wall-mounted TVs have only one channel. It is not *Fox News.*
- Parents watch the TVs more than they watch their babies.
- The office girls who call up the patients are impossible to understand.
- And, you can add your list of another 20 items yourself.

It is only fair to acknowledge that waiting rooms are an absolute necessity. It is better that patients are seated there instead of waiting in their cars in the small parking lots.

And, most important, waiting rooms are usually located near doctors' exam rooms, but they are 200 yards down a dark hall from the MRI and CT scan machines, a quarter-mile from any bathroom, and a half-mile from a drinking fountain. I firmly believe that there are at least 40 waiting rooms and waiting areas in every hospital or medical center. In office buildings---specifically built for doctors---there are up to seven waiting rooms on every floor.

And, let's not overlook the magazine departments. There are several types of magazine areas:

- One pile contains only magazines with the address label having been cut away.
- Another contains only *WebMD* magazines, all last month's issues. Or last year's.
- Another contains only *Texas Highways, Texas Monthly, Texas Roadhouses*---and that waiting area is located in waiting rooms in New Mexico. Or maybe Chihuahua.
- One section is very orderly and has a compartment for each magazine. It is always located in an inaccessible

location, usually behind the cashier. Most are Latino titles.
- There is seldom a current daily newspaper. ¿El Diario?

During these past 30 months, I have become a fixture in waiting rooms for:

- <u>Doctor Kevin Bright</u>. It is always clean and decorated timely for seasonal holidays. I estimate I have been there 30 times. I even have my own private, flowery chair.
- <u>Doctors at Texas Oncology West Side</u>. It is always full of patients, and its coffee pot is usually empty or the coffee cold. With two of my doctors located there, I estimate I have been there 50 times.
- <u>Doctors at Texas Oncology East Side</u>. Large lobby waiting room area. I have been there three times for PET scans, but that ought to be a separate chapter. Or not.
- <u>Doctor Ben Matthew, my cardiologist at El Paso Heart Center</u>. It is very large and has vending machines for sodas, candy and chips. Huh? In a heart center? Its TV is pre-set, and it is not *Fox News*. I have answered the roll call there about 20 times.
- <u>Major hospitals</u>. There are multiple waiting rooms at Sierra Medical Center, Providence Medical Center, and Las Palmas Medical Center—for pre-registration, registration, out-patient services, in-patient services, cashier desks, insurance counters, the medical director, and the cafeteria. There are no waiting rooms for the elevators. Counting all the times for CT scans, ultrasounds, etc., I have been in waiting rooms at all three hospitals at least 15 times. Probably more.
- <u>Diagnostic Out-patient Imaging Clinic</u>. Very friendly staff and an excellent ice-cold drinking fountain, smaller waiting areas outside the CT scan room, the

MRI room, the ultrasound room, and an exam room with a bed where Dr. William Boushka performed a needle-biopsy on me at the outset of my health issues. I keep hoping my waiting room days are winding down. But I doubt it. As long as the doctors on my medical roster call me back for another appointment---and Medicare and Mutual of Omaha continue to help with expenses---I'll see you there . . . waiting next to the Volkswagen beetle, blocking the aisle.

* * *

AUTHOR'S NOTE: *Every appointment, exam, surgery, and treatment described in this book took place in El Paso, Texas. It is the city where I was born, and where I reside today. Recently, a nationwide poll showed that the "friendliest" city in the U.S. is El Paso. Yes, El Paso, Texas!*

I cannot speak about every "friendly" person here, but I can speak about all those orderlies, clerks, nurses, and doctors that I describe on these pages---all of them, without exception--- could not be more "friendly." And helpful. I can vouch for that.

PART ONE

"YOU'VE GOT CANCER"

THE THREE WORDS WE DREAD
OUR DOCTOR SAYING

Chapter One

TIME FOR A DIAGNOSIS

ONCE YOU GET PAST Merriam-Webster's initial definition of "cancer" which deals with the "northern zodiacal constellation between Gemini and Leo," you get right down to the real, more earthly meaning:

"A malignant tumor of potentially unlimited growth that expands locally by invasion and systematically by metastasis."

The dictionary goes on, adding:

"An abnormal state marked by such tumors---a source of evil and anguish."

That about sums it up. Cancer is not a foreign word to those of us past middle age, some of us way past. Chances are one of your loved ones or a close friend or someone you know has had cancer, been treated for cancer, or even died of cancer. You, yourself, may have cancer or have been treated for it. But, let's hope not.

I have not been so lucky. On two different occasions---once in 1985 and again in 1992---I had what Dr. John Pate called a sublingual mass removed from under my tongue. Obviously, it returned after the first time but I have had no problem since the 1992 recurrence. Doctor Pate, who performed both procedures, has even quit practicing oral surgery and has changed his practice to plastic surgery. He did a good job for me.

But time moves on.

I am writing portions of this book in diary form---sort of day-to-day---as my current experience as a recent cancer patient moves forward. The diagnosis of what I have now is not a sublingual mass; it is cancer, pure and simple. Should this become your lot, I hope what I am writing here will help you through this *"abnormal state---the source of evil and anguish,"* as Merriam-Webster defines it.

* * *

No Serious Health Issues

I have never been a health freak. I try to take care of myself: I quit smoking cigarettes 40 years ago and I haven't missed them at all. And I quit beer and the hard stuff almost 15 years ago although I occasionally gulp down a Guinness stout when I feel Irish. I exercise very little since I quit playing golf four years ago when arthritis in my hands made it difficult to hit a ball without pain. My wife, Mary, and I have a treadmill and an exercise machine which I notice from time to time but rarely use. I eat and drink things I like: Mexican food, salmon, Irish soda-bread, pastry, ice cream, diet sodas and Mexican food (or did I mention tamales, enchiladas, and . . .).

I am diabetic, controlled by prescriptions. My heart has been okay with no problems.

On a morning in 2012, I notice a lump on the right side of my neck and I decide to have a doctor take a look at it. So, this is where all my medical issues begin:

* * *

August 20, 2012. I am in an examination room in the offices of Dr. Humberto Serna, a nephrologist and the husband of my primary care physician, Dr. Aime Serna. She has sent me here because the creatinine reading from my latest blood work was 1.35 and that is out of range. She is concerned that I may be entering the second stage of renal failure. I have no idea how many stages there are to renal failure, but there must be several because no one seems in a panic. Dr. Humberto is a soft spoken Latino who has either Cuban or Puerto Rican ancestry, and he is genuinely interested in my condition. I like his "bedside" manner.

He tells me I am not drinking enough water. He says three half-liter bottles would be about right. *And, he adds, "Lay off the caffeine-free Diet Cokes."* He wants to see me again in about six weeks and tells his nurse to make the appointment.

"Oh. One other thing, doctor," I remark in conclusion. "I have this lump on the right side of my neck. It doesn't hurt, but I just noticed it about a month ago." He looks it over and feels it. *"Let's get you an appointment with Dr. Bright. His office is in the next building down the street."*

"I'll get the appointment myself, doctor, but thanks for the suggestion."

Dr. Humberto's nurse escorts me to the appointment counter.

"See you in six weeks," the medical assistant says.

* * *

And, When You Grow Old . . .

I am an 85-year-old white male, Caucasian of Irish descent, and in relatively good health for my age. I take a few prescription drugs for various ailments but none too serious. My blood sugar is high enough to rank me as a diabetic, but I have kept it under control most of the time with Janumet, a highly-prescribed combination of Januvia and metformin (glucophage). Shortly before the appointment with Doctor Humberto, Doctor Aime Serna had just taken me off Janumet and switched me over to Januvia, eliminating the glucophage which I understand is bad for kidneys.

As I wrote earlier, I take fairly good care of myself: I am six feet three inches tall, weigh 195 pounds, have recently quit playing golf because of arthritis in my hands. I quit drinking years ago when I had a pancreas scare, but will drink a glass of chardonnay on rare occasions . . . if the company is right. I quit smoking years ago. I've got a little stomach paunch, but still short of a pot belly. I am virtually retired from our supermarket business because my son, Joseph, is aggressive and up-to-date managing the stores while I am more passive and "old school," which is not recommended in today's fast-moving retail food business. Mary is my wife for over 40 years. She is a licensed vocational nurse and, like me, is retired and loves to play golf. She is younger than me---a lively 79-year-old care-giver who is determined that I will outlive Methuselah, even if it kills her doing so.

* * *

September 7, 2012. I have a stubborn nosebleed and decide it is time to have my nasal passages cauterized. And, I need to check on that lump in my neck. I try to get an appointment with Dr. Kevin Bright whom Dr. Humberto suggested, but the first available date is the last week of October because he will be out of the office or is scheduled up until then. So, I call Dr. R.A.D. Morton, a well-respected ear, nose, and throat specialist who has practiced in El Paso for many years. I am able to get in in two weeks.

September 20, 2012. Doctor Morton and I are not contemporaries, but we share some mutual friends. We talk about the good old days in high school and the rivalry between his El Paso High Tigers and my Austin High Panthers. Then he cauterizes one nasal passage, and I bring to his attention the lump in the neck. He feels it, and then quickly recommends that I go to Providence Medical Center across the street from his office.

"Have some blood work performed, and have a CT scan," he states.

He says to do it now. During the next three or four hours, I register in, go to a waiting room, have blood drawn, go to another waiting room, and finally have the CT scan. Once I am on the moveable table inside the machine, it is a brief exam. The technician will send the report to Doctor Morton.

October 1, 2012. Doctor Morton calls me into his office. No small talk this time.

"It looks like a squamous cell carcinoma to me," he says, "and you need to get rid of it right away. I don't do surgery anymore because I am not as steady as I used to be, but I am going to send you to Doctor Bright who is an excellent surgeon. He'll take care of it."

Mary and I drive directly to Doctor Bright's office, plead for a prompt appointment because we have plans for a two-week European cruise scheduled to leave London October 13th.

* * *

A Time for Wine

Back in May, we decided to take a two-week cruise along the western coast of Europe on what Celebrity Cruises calls an Immersive Wine Cruise. I am not sure what an immersive wine cruise is, but it sounds like something we would enjoy, it is reasonably priced (if a cruise can be reasonably priced), and it works into our fall schedule. We use air miles with Delta for round-trip tickets to London, leaving El Paso on October 12th, and use more air miles with Hilton Hotels so we can stay an extra night and fly out of London back home on October 26th.

* * *

October 8, 2012. Doctor Bright listens to the events that brought us to his office, and then is able to pull up my CT scan of September 20th onto his in-office computer. He then performs a scope procedure in which a small tube runs through my nose into my throat, and a camera at the end of the tube records my nose, throat, and everything else along the way. He is watching a monitor showing him what the camera is photographing, and then he is able to show it to me from the recording it made.

He agrees with Doctor Morton's diagnosis, but wants to have a needle-biopsy of the carcinoma in my neck before he decides on surgery. He is sympathetic to our concern about the scheduled air flight and wine cruise, and says that we should continue with our plans because another two weeks will not make any difference if surgery is necessary. He believes he will have the result of the needle-biopsy by October 11th, the day before we are scheduled to fly to London.

October 9, 2012. I go to Diagnostic Out-Patient Imaging Clinic, register in, show the registrar my health insurance cards and driver's license, wait a short while, and then am escorted to a large exam room. Shortly, Doctor Boushka, a radiologist who owns the place, has a few pleasant things to say to me, gets me in the right position on a bed, and injects a special needle into the lump. It is painless and quickly done.

October 11, 2012. Doctor Bright calls to inform us that the needle-biopsy confirms that the lump is a squamous cell carcinoma, and that he will make all arrangements for surgery

Author John Welsh and wife Mary try to enjoy a Celebrity Cruise after being told of John's cancer and upcoming radiation and chemotherapy treatments.

at Providence Medical Center to be performed when we return. He instructs me to make an appointment with Dr. Anuradha Gupta, a board certified radiation-oncologist, for October 29th, the Monday after our return from the cruise. In conclusion, he says for us to enjoy the cruise, and that he will contact us on November 5th to inform us of the time of surgery.

October 12, 2012. We fly out of El Paso at 6 a.m., non-stop to Atlanta where we have a five-hour layover before the flight to London. We pledge to one another to have a good time and, besides that, the lump in my neck has not changed, it seems. We have told no one about the cancer or the upcoming surgery. No one includes friends and family.

*   *   *

A Serious Accident, but All Survive

What follows stretches the imagination: these things cannot be happening to one family. That's what I thought.

Our son Joseph's (then) 14-year-old son Patrick graduated from St. Clement's Parish School this past June and was accepted for high school at St. Paul's School in Concord, NH. St. Paul's was the family's first choice of the five Northeastern boarding schools we visited last year, and Patrick was fortunate to receive a four-year scholarship with only minimal cost to his family. Patrick's family---Father Joseph, Mother Liliana, Brother Nathan (12), and Sister Carling (4) flew to Boston on October 11th, rented a car and drove the short distance to Concord for Parent's Week-End at St. Paul's.

As our layover in Atlanta nears its end, I call Joseph to find out how the visit is going because it is Patrick's first time away from home alone, and his family's first time away from Patrick for any length of time. When I inquire to Joseph, he responds:

"Dad, I hadn't planned on telling you this because I don't want to ruin your trip, but we were in a serious car wreck last night."

Joseph tells me what happened: As they were exiting a freeway at Concord, their car was struck from behind by a huge suburban vehicle---a Tahoe---which had been altered with larger tires and the body of the vehicle jacked up. The impact shoved their car's rear bumper and back seat against the front seat. Although Joseph and Liliana were only bruised and bumped around, the children were seriously injured and were rushed by ambulance to the Concord hospital. After an initial examination, Nathan was airlifted to Boston Children's Hospital. He suffered a fractured skull, his facial bones were broken and pushed out of place, and his left eye socket and optic nerve were damaged. Carling's right ear was lacerated--- almost totally cut off---but was successfully re-attached at the Concord hospital.

At this point, I tell Joseph that we will change our flight, cancel the cruise, and catch another plane to Boston and should be there within a few hours; but he is adamant about continuing our trip:

"There is nothing you can do here. I have things under control. You go ahead. We will keep in touch by email as things develop," he says.

He accepts no other decision. So, with this horrible accident having just occurred and my diagnosis of cancer and upcoming surgery, we reluctantly agree, and soon board our flight to London. I say nothing to Joseph about my cancer.

Aftermath: Liliana and Carling flew back to El Paso on the Monday following the Thursday night accident for further examination and any necessary treatment from an audiologist. Nathan was discharged from Boston Children's Hospital on October 20th after brain surgery, facial reconstruction, and treatment of his left eye optic nerve. He stayed in a Boston hotel with his Dad, and made daily appointments at the hospital, treated by three top-notch surgeons who also teach at nearby Harvard Medical School. He and Joseph returned to El Paso on November 4th, and Nathan was greeted by a large group of classmates, AAU basketball teammates, many friends, and some media people who filmed the airport arrival and told the local television audience about the accident and his treatments.

At the time of this writing, he has recovered most of his vision in his left eye and from the substantial bruising on his face. He now wears contact lenses and is back playing basketball.

* * *

October 29, 2012. On the Monday following our return from the European cruise, we meet with Doctor Gupta, a highly-respected radiation-oncologist. So far, she seems to have a pleasant way with patients. She tells you what is wrong and what can be done about it, and what you will go through during the treatment. She doesn't mince words, but creates a feeling of trust and confidence. She is highly thought of by her peers.

During our absence, she has reviewed both the earlier CT scan and results of the needle-biopsy. She says the cancer in the neck is not the "mother" cancer, in her words, and that it is likely there is another cancer elsewhere in my body. She says a PET scan would give us the answer, and that she had scheduled one for the following Friday, November 2nd.

November 2, 2012. The PET scan is like a CT scan on steroids. I lay on the moveable bed while my body stutters through the round donut-looking apparatus which contains series of cameras. My head is secured, and blankets keep my arms and body fixed in place. The technician wants no movement. My problem is I have a cough. The machine moves every four minutes and the cameras continue to click away. I need to cough. Badly. Finally I do cough, and the technician stops the machine, reviews the pictures it has taken, and says everything is okay. It starts up again. The procedure lasts almost 40 minutes, but it seems like months.

November 5, 2012. The results of the PET scan are in Doctor Gupta's hands when we arrive for our appointment at 10:30

a.m. She explains that the mother cancer is located at the base of my tongue, and that the only way it can be treated is with a combination of radiation and chemotherapy. She details the several steps we have to go through before treatment can begin. The cancer cannot be removed by surgery because it is near my voice box and esophagus.

First, she says, a biopsy of the mother cancer will be taken instead of the planned removal of the cancerous lump in my neck during the surgery scheduled for tomorrow. It is a procedure similar to an endoscopy: a tube is inserted down the throat and a biopsy is taken of a small piece of the cancer at the base of my tongue.

Next, she says, will be a dental examination and a fitting for a fluoridation tray. Because of the radiation treatment to follow, my teeth and mouth must be in decent condition to handle the intensity of the radiation. After that, I will consult with a gastroenterologist who, in the next few days, will insert a feeding tube into my stomach so that I can receive proper nutrition since it will be difficult to swallow during the treatments. The gastroenterologist will also recommend a home care nurse to teach Mary how to prepare food for placement into the feeding tube.

Doctor Gupta says the radiation-chemo treatment will begin after she gets a green light from the dentist, and that the feeding tube is either inserted or is about to be inserted.

Later that day, I meet with Joseph and Liliana to bring them up-to-date on my condition. Earlier, I had told Joseph about the lump in my neck, but I had not told him that it was cancer. While I tell him about the cancer, he has his head lowered, looking at his cell phone. Outwardly, he displays no feeling one way or the other. Both he and Liliana say nothing.

Chapter Two

PREPARING FOR TREATMENT

THERE IS A LOT OF preparation that I must go through before the treatments can begin: the biopsy surgery, the dental examination and any dental work needed, another surgery to insert the stomach tube, and enough time to pass for the dental work to heal. It is time to begin.

November 6, 2012. The outpatient surgery goes off without a hitch, and I am released from the hospital within a few hours. I am sore from the tube in my throat, my lips are slightly bruised, and there is minor pain in my throat which I believe is from the biopsy. Doctor Bright performs the surgery.

Joseph calls. He says he is going to vote and that he and Liliana will be at our house after that. Joseph could be no clearer: I have his total support, and he wants to be a part of any decisions we make. Without me knowing it, Mary asks Joseph to inform his two older brothers who live elsewhere. He responds that he will take care of that.

November 9, 2012. The dental exam turns into a nightmare. My dentist, who has seen me for over ten years and is well aware of my dental problems, says I have mobility in two teeth and gum disease in two others, all on the left side (the radiation will be concentrated on the right side of my neck and throat). Dr. Bill Jabalie, the dentist, says he has had one other patient with a similar problem, and that the patient went through some tough times: no saliva, continual mouth sores, loss of skin inside the mouth, loss of skin from the tongue. He warns that I need to understand what all the side effects will be and, further, that if the teeth are not removed, then I will be susceptible to loss of jawbone. The picture he paints is not pretty. For the first time since this entire episode began, I become somewhat emotional. I begin to wonder whether I should proceed with the treatment. After all---I try to convince myself---the tongue cancer does not cause pain, and we can have Doctor Bright remove the cancer in my neck, and then everything will be okay.

Mary is upset as well. She repeats several times she does not want me to have to go through all the pain that the dentist has described. If things get worse, we can always have the radiation-chemo treatment. And I agree. We think we will just wait to hear what Doctor Gupta says when we discuss our apprehension with her during our appointment on November 12th, the following Monday.

I hint to Joseph and close friends that I might forego the radiation-chemo treatment. Joseph says he will accompany us to the appointment with Doctor Gupta.

Patient John Welsh received radiation and chemotherapy at Texas Oncology Center, West El Paso location, which also contains offices of Dr. Panagoitis Valilis and Dr. Anuradha Gupta.

November 12, 2012. Doctor Gupta is almost aghast that I had not had the dental work done, and that we had cancelled our appointment with the gastroenterologist for the stomach tube. When I explain that I am considering not following through with the treatment she had outlined, she comes right to the point. She says I need to understand that I am going to have the pain and the difficulty in swallowing whether we have the radiation or not. She says the tongue cancer will continue to grow, and that it has been there probably for only a few months. She is clear: I have a 65 percent chance of getting rid of the cancer and leading a normal life, but that is compared to being on a morphine drip with no chance of surviving the cancer without treatment. Now, everyone in the room---Mary, Joseph, and Doctor Gupta---have their eyes squarely on me.

It is my decision, it is now time to decide. I have made many tough decisions in my life---concerning my family, my career, my business, all those things---but nothing like this one. It boils down to this: it is a matter of choosing to have a good chance to live or choosing to have a certain result of death. When I realize what the choices really are, I say we should go ahead with the treatment.

Everyone is relieved, and probably no one any more so than Doctor Gupta. She tells us to reschedule the gastroenterologist appointment, to have the dental work done, and then she would proceed with the radiation treatment two weeks after the teeth are removed. She arranges a meeting within a few hours with the chemo-oncologist, Dr. Panagiotis Valilis, whose office is located in the same Texas Oncology building.

Doctor Valilis has already studied all my recent medical records. Because of my kidney problem, he says he will not be treating me with standard chemotherapy, but instead will be infusing me once a week with a relatively new treatment, a drug named Erbitux. He says it will not cause nausea or hair loss, and the only side effect might be diarrhea. He plans for the first infusion to coincide with the beginning of radiation, two weeks after the dental work.

November 13, 2012. It takes Doctor Jabalie about 90 minutes to complete his dental work. Only one of the four teeth proves difficult to remove because it continues to break as he attempts to pull it out. He writes out a prescription for some pain pills, but it turns out that I have little or no pain from the extractions. Now the radiation and chemo can begin in two weeks.

November 15, 2012. My gastroenterologist, Dr. Verkat Kolli, explains the feeding tube procedure. I will check in at a local hospital where my stomach will be cleaned out thoroughly. He compares the placement of the feeding tube into my stomach with an electrician pulling wire from one outlet to the breaker panel. I immediately feel the wire with a hook on the end! He says the tube will be smaller than his little finger, and will protrude about ten inches outside my body. I will have to stay overnight at the hospital. I guess that will wind up all the prelim activity so that the radiation-chemo can begin.

November 16, 2012. Mary has a wonderful singing voice. Wherever we have lived, she has joined the church choir. She sings solos, or duets, whatever. Back in the mid-1990s when we were on a seven-month sabbatical, living in Ireland, she joined the cast of a local musical group, and sang a solo on RTE, the Ireland national television and radio network, when the program was shown across the island country. Her Irish church choir at St. Mary's competed in a major choir competition in Wales while we were in Ireland. She sings at funerals or weddings when asked. She just loves to sing. And, yes, she sometimes sings in the shower.

She also loves to hum, but I had to call her out on the humming this morning. I was feeling somewhat depressed about my condition and feeling some pain in my throat, and she was humming *"When the Roll Is Called Up Yonder."*

*   *   *

The Husband-Wife Bond

My outward reaction to all this has been sort of "laid back." I want to appear tough and able to handle all the pain and trauma that is soon to arrive, and be a model patient for the doctors and nurses. I especially don't want to affect Mary's life and that of other members of our family. I want and need their support, but I don't want sympathy. I want to be tough and handle this like . . . well, a man. I don't know what my emotions will become as the treatment nears and the final result unknown. Right now I am a little depressed, but I don't know if feeling weak is just in my mind, or is the result of the cancer growing and the problem increasing. I guess time will tell.

On Saturday evening, November 10th, our hot water heater started leaking, and Mary slips on the wet floor tile, falls and breaks her right arm at the wrist. The physician's assistant at the emergency room does not set the break properly, and our orthopedic doctor will have to pin the broken bones during an out-patient surgery next week. Mary is still a nurse---broken arm and all---but cannot do everything she would normally do around the house. So I have to help with those things she cannot do for herself, such as opening a can of dog food, fastening her bra, drying her off after she showers, putting on and adjusting the rib belt she has to wear to relieve pain from three broken ribs she also sustained when she fell. It is very uncomfortable for her: carrying her broken arm at an angle in the cast and sling, enduring the pain she feels from the sling around her neck, and not being able to tend to me like she would otherwise.

But, if you look deep enough, you can always find something good in every bad situation: helping her with her broken wrist takes my mind off my own problems. Times like these are what tighten the bonds between husband and wife.

* * *

November 16, 2012. I have a late afternoon appointment with Doctor Gupta, but I assume she is running overtime with earlier-scheduled patients because Mary and I are over an hour behind our appointment when the nurse calls me in to take my vitals. Doctor Gupta gets an update on our appointments: she asks for the details of Doctor Kolli's schedule to insert the feeding tube, and examines my mouth to check on the extractions. She remarks that there needs to be more healing, but with the two weeks delay before the radiation begins, there will be plenty of time.

She then sets a schedule of her own: on Monday, November 26th, I will be fitted for the mask that I must wear during the radiation treatments. Then, on Wednesday, November 28th, I will go through another fitting of the mask during which she will mark the exact locations where the radiation will be aimed; then, the following day, I will have the first treatment, and radiation will then proceed Monday through Friday for the next six-plus weeks.

*   *   *

The Man in the Plastic Mask

The two young men who will fit my mask seem very well-trained, and are very courteous to their new patient. I am escorted into a large room that houses another one of those huge machines that have a gigantic mechanism for patient radiation treatment. Like all the others, it appears to have cameras or something that will do something to the mask when the time comes. The lead technician shows me one of the masks that he will fit over the front and sides of my head, my face, my neck, and my upper chest. The mask is white plastic, perforated with a million holes, and is still flat at this time. He explains that he will soak the mask in warm water, lay it over my head, face, neck, and chest and will then apply pressure everywhere to make it form-fitting.

The technicians attach a cloth sling to each wrist and pull my arms down toward my feet. The lead guy explains that they don't want my shoulders to move upward during the fitting, so

they tie them down to prevent movement. It smarts a little. I facetiously ask:
"When does the water-boarding begin?" *They laugh at the dark humor; I grimace.*
My head is placed stationary on the narrow table, and the mask feels warm. I am told to close my eyes so that water cannot drip into them. I try to breathe normally, but that is not easy. The table moves forward and backward, I think, several times. After a period that seems like two months, I am told there will be another 20 minutes. I grimace. Again.
But, everything ends sometime. Finally, the machine grinds to a stop, the wrist slings are removed, and I am helped off the table onto my feet. The lead guy is proud to show me my mask; it looks like a Toys R Us facial skeleton with miniscule bones and lots of holes. I look at it closely and remark:
"Ugly bastard, isn't it?" *They laugh again at my attempt to be funny.*
The mask contains several little tabs marked with an X, which I assume is the ultimate aiming point.
"The doctor will adjust the markings when you return Wednesday," he explains. "Then you will be on the table a little longer than you were today . . . in fact, it will be the longest preparation you will have . . . a little less than an hour." *Another grimace.*
As Mary and I gather our jackets and papers, I think to myself that I am actually looking forward to the radiation treatments to begin because I am growing weary of all the appointments and all the prep work and all the time spent mindlessly thumbing through outdated magazines in the waiting rooms. I try to be patient through all of this, and I completely understand why there are always delays in doctors' appointments. Each patient requires a different amount of time than another, and all doctors want to give their undivided attention to their patient during their exam time. But their cell phones ring with calls from another doctor or they are asked questions by the nurses and medical assistants. All this

is necessary, I am sure, but the effect is always an extended time in the waiting room for the next patient. I wonder why they don't schedule a little more time between appointments.

* * *

November 19, 2012. I have a previously-scheduled appointment with Dr. Humberto Serna, and he reviews the results of the blood work he has requested. The creatinine reading is slightly down and he is happy about that, feeling the increased amount of water I am drinking has helped.

I inform him about the cancer and he wants the full story. He is pleased with the oncologists who will be treating me, and especially since Doctor Valilis will be using Erbitux as my chemotherapy. He backs up Doctor Valilis' concern about the standard chemo damaging kidneys of those patients with those problems.

* * *

A Short Break with the Family

Our El Paso family has established a tradition of spending three or four days around Thanksgiving every year at the Hyatt Regency Tamaya Resort north of Albuquerque. We leave tomorrow after Mary's broken wrist is reset and pins inserted, and we will meet Joseph, Liliana, Patrick, Nathan, and Carling early evening. Mary's sister Sue Gregory and her two daughters, two granddaughters, a grandson, a son-in-law and one of the granddaughters' boyfriend will all join us on Wednesday night for the annual get-together. They all live in Santa Fe. Another couple and their two sons, friends from El Paso, also join in.

Joseph has reserved a large suite with two adjoining bedrooms, and it is perfect to entertain this many folks. He has made certain there is adequate drink and food---we have a great time.

Each of Sue's group knows about my cancer diagnosis, and it is interesting to me to observe how they treat me and what they have to say . . . particularly at the end of the evening when they are leaving. The younger ones all mention that I will be in their prayers, and that they are confident things will go well. Sue, who is in the midst of treatment for breast cancer herself, brings me up-to-date on her experience with the chemo and another drug she is taking without her doctor's knowledge. Of course, she is recommending it to me. I don't think so. The few days around Thanksgiving has helped getting my mind off the events to come next week. I spend as much time as possible with Patrick and Nathan, but these young boys are much more into their iPhones and iPads than any meaningful conversation with their grandfather. Nevertheless, we do talk a lot about basketball and St. Paul's School and Nathan's tutoring. All in all, it has been a fun three days, and we all look forward to returning to Tamaya next year.

*   *   *

November 26, 2012. I pick up my fluoridation trays today from Doctor Jabalie. He tells me the twice-a-day fluoride treatment is a procedure I need to plan on following for the rest of my life. It only takes a few minutes to do, but he says it will help reduce cavities, and that it is important because my mouth and gums will be taking a beating during the radiation and chemo treatments. He also prescribes fluoride toothpaste to compliment the treatment with the trays---which are a very thin, clear plastic mold of all my teeth---easily filled with fluoride, placed atop my teeth, and removed after about five minutes.

He says the spaces where he removed the four teeth two weeks ago are healing nicely, and that the slight pain I have with my jaw will disappear within a few more days. The office visit today winds up all the preliminaries; those dealing with my cancer are still a few days away.

The stomach surgery takes place at Sierra Medical Center, and the pre-registration office obtains my insurance information and reminds me to bring Doctor Kolli's orders with me when I report at 7:30 a.m. tomorrow. I will be staying overnight and should be released mid-morning Wednesday, November 28th.

November 27, 2012. I go through the usual hospital admission procedures and I notice there seems to be a shortage of patient care employees, even though all are patient-friendly. They put me through the pre-op steps which include a complete cleaning of my stomach and, after a short wait, the anesthesiologist does his job. I won't feel a thing, he says, that I'll probably hear the orders and comments of the doctors and nurses, and that the whole thing won't last long. Doctor Kolli arrives and the operation gets underway.

It doesn't take long, and then I am taken to a recovery room while the anesthesia wears off and . . . when the nurses agree that it has . . . I am wheeled to my private room. I quickly fall asleep. An orderly brings me a tray of food, and I eat some of it through my mouth. Then I fall asleep again.

I have a drip solution of something---I assume it is to keep me from dehydration---and it hangs from an IV pole with wheels. During the night I have to urinate. I have to move the IV pole with me into the bathroom close to my bed. During this "adventure," I somehow twist my knee . . . and it hurts . . . but I make it back to my bed without falling. I am uncomfortable, but I position myself in the bed so it bothers me less.

The next morning the knee is swollen substantially. After the nurses check me over---I can't recall whether Doctor Kolli or someone else cleared me for discharge---an orderly wheels me to the front door, and Mary is there to drive me home. The swollen knee is a problem; I can't walk without help. We have my late mother-in-law's walker in the garage, Mary cleans it up, and I use it around the house to prevent a fall. What a day: surgery *and* a damaged knee.

November 28, 2012. Doctor Gupta finishes putting her aim-point onto the mask and asks me about the walker and my swollen knee. I tell her Mary has already made me an appointment with Dr. Don Klein, an orthopedic physician, for that afternoon. Doctor Gupta reminds me about tomorrow's first radiation treatment.

Mary has an appointment with another doctor to check on her broken wrist and cast, and we ask a close friend, Sheryll Van Pelt, to drive us to the orthopedic group's offices about 20 miles across El Paso so I can see Doctor Klein about my knee, and Mary can see Dr. John Dickason about her broken wrist which he reset. Doctor Klein drains the fluid off my knee, and the walker helps me to get from his examining room to our friend's car without falling.

I don't know what else can happen to keep me from beginning the radiation treatment set to begin at 5:30 p.m. tomorrow. But I remember Murphy's Law . . .

Chapter Three

THE TREATMENT BEGINS

MARY AND I ARRIVE at Doctor Gupta's office at the Texas Oncology building just before 5:30 p.m. on November 29th. It is already dark outside, and the waiting room still holds several patients. AJ Sharmay, one of the two radiation technicians, takes me from the waiting room to a small dressing room, assigns me one of the empty lockers, and tells me to undress down to my underwear and put on one of those gowns that you tie in the back and hold closed so you won't expose your . . . underwear.

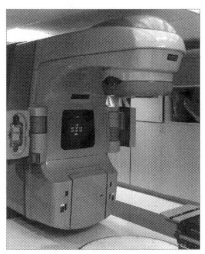

The radiation machine at Texas Oncology Center.
The radiation-oncologist determines the aim-point for the
radiation and it is marked on either the patient's mask
or body. The back portion of the machine is stationary,
and the front portion rotates around the patient.

After I get the gown in place, AJ leads me down a couple of corridors into a large room what holds the huge radiation machine. He positions me on the moveable table-bed, and places my mask over my head, my face, my neck, and my upper chest. He fastens the mask to the bed. He tells me the radiation treatment will take about 20 minutes. He says the machine will perform 18 separate treatments as it rotates around my head and neck. Janice Dieter, another technician, covers me with a blanket because it is cool in the radiation room. My apprehension about what will happen is almost gone, and AJ and Janice leave the room, enter an adjoining control room, and start the procedure. *I think "Oh, well, here goes!"*

* * *

Reality Settles In

I suppose there is always apprehension when something new is about to begin. Especially if it has to do with your health and well-being, and you are an old guy like me. But I am determined to see this through, and reality is finally fixed in my mind. I find it hard to understand, however, how cancer found me after all these years. And I know for certain that many people are praying for my recovery, and I am praying that God will hear---and answer---their prayers, as well as mine. Does all this sound selfish? I hope not.

* * *

November 28, 2012. The sound of a big machine running tells me the radiation treatment is underway. There is no music, only that whirling noise. The part of the machine that is emitting the radiation moves slowly from one side of my head, face, and neck and then to the other side. I can't see much of what is taking place above my head, but the whirling goes suddenly quiet and it is obvious that it is now located where Doctor Gupta and her technicians have programmed it to stop.

The machine then continues its designated course and, after a few rotations, I can almost predict where it is in relation to my head. Repeating its course seems to make the time pass a little quicker, and then the machine quits. AJ tells me it is over, moves the table-bed about six feet out, Janice removes the blanket, and they both help me to sit up and regain my balance before I grab my walker.

AJ walks beside me back down the same corridors to the dressing room so I can get out of the gown and put on my own clothes. Mary is up on her feet waiting for me as I shuffle down the hall, and she leads me to the car. It is 7 p. m., and I am bushed, dead tired. I tell her---the best I can remember--- what all happened with the radiation. I tell her I felt pretty good about this first treatment, and what apprehension remained is gone. I hope forever.

Now I can look forward to the first chemo treatment tomorrow.

November 30, 2012. My first day of chemo begins at 9:45 a.m. with the lab work, then I move to the treatment rooms upstairs. There are dozens of lazy-boy type chairs spaced out along the walls, complete with guest chairs alongside. Mary can sit beside me. My nurse tells me that this first treatment will last for three hours, not two like the remaining six. The nurse says I am dehydrated and I will have to have the saline solution infused before the chemo is administered.

She carefully monitors the drip, drip, drip of the IV into my left arm. I watch the bag empty its contents at the same speed as Egyptians building a pyramid. It is drip . . . drip . . . drip, and then she changes the bag from the saline solution to the Erbitux chemo that Doctor Valilis promised would not cost me my already-balding grey hair.

The chemo solution looks the same as the saline solution did. Clear. Same speed. Drip, drip, drip. My nurse monitors the same as she did earlier, and time continues to drag on.

Somehow my schedule has become screwed up because my second radiation treatment is supposed to begin at 12:10 p.m., following the chemo. But I don't get out of the chemo treatment until after 2 p.m. The late start of chemo causes the delay, but it turns out okay in the end because it is painless, and that is a relief. My first chemo treatment is history.

AJ and Janice are waiting for me in the radiation area downstairs. I follow the same procedure as yesterday, and we finish up at about 4 p.m. Mary and I wind up the two treatments, and they take six hours. An awfully long day. We're both pooped. And it's just the first day . . .

The white plastic mask indicates patient is about to receive radiation. The mask covers his head, face, neck, and upper chest and is fastened to the bed-table to prevent movement. In this case, the machine rotates around the patient's upper body. If cancer is elsewhere, aim-point is changed.

*   *   *

My "Entrees:" IsoSource and Gatorade

With the Thursday and Friday treatments behind me, now I can look forward to a two-day break over the week-end. My knee is somewhat better, but I am still a little unstable so I continue to use the walker. To help my energy to stay as high as possible, I am drinking Gatorade---seven bottles over the week-end. Mary is feeding me a high-calorie liquid supplement named IsoSource through the stomach tube. It is recommended by Tender Care Home Health. Each bottle is 375 calories and Mary pumps six bottles into me each day, exceeding a 2000-calories diet needed for adequate nutrition. The IsoSource is delivered in lots of eight cases, each containing 24 bottles, by a local medical supply company, and its cost is paid by Medicare and Mutual of Omaha insurance. It is supposed to be consumed only through a stomach tube. It is labelled "Vanilla," but it is tasteless since it goes directly into my stomach.

The Gatorade keeps me awake at night and, after I talk to Doctor Aime Serna about this, she prescribes a sleeping pill, and that does the job. I sleep like a baby. Chewing and swallowing is another problem---and that's the reason for the liquid diet. The radiation has caused this, but Mary insists I try to eat solid foods. But I can't swallow foods that I can chew; they just won't go down.

* * *

December 3, 2012. I have an early morning appointment with Doctor Klein for a check-up on my knee. He says it is okay, and that I can abandon the walker after tomorrow, if I feel comfortable without it. I try a cane, but it does not give me the stability and confidence that I need to keep from falling.

The radiation and chemo treatments continue and another infusion of saline solution is needed because I am dehydrated. I don't know why because I am drinking several bottles of water through the day because my mouth is so dry. I guess the radiation is beginning to affect my saliva glands.

After my third chemo treatment my face begins to look like a teenager's. I am showing pimples and a red rash. And, after the fourth chemo infusion, Doctors Gupta and Valilis confer and decide to stop the Erbitux chemo because of the reaction. With the possibility of damage to my kidneys, there is no other chemo I can take. However, Doctor Valilis wants to continue to see me on a regular weekly basis. I am okay with that because Doctor Valilis has his laboratory draw blood just before each visit so that he will have full results before the exam ends. He studies the blood report very thoroughly because he doesn't want any more surprises. The pimples disappear within a few days.

After a few more radiation treatments, the two oncologists decide that a two-week break is in order, and I will begin the radiation again on January 2nd. The break is welcome because Christmas is a few days away, and that means chaos with the grandchildren bouncing off the walls with anticipation. The Christmas tree and all the decorations are in place, and the tree lights are working. But as far as Mary and I are concerned, it is somewhat different than Christmas a year ago.

January 2, 2013. Radiation treatments take up all of January. It is five days a week, usually mid-morning, and takes the normal 20 minutes plus the time in the waiting room. Even though it is routine now and still pain free, I can tell I am losing strength and stability. I am not the same guy who began these treatments last December, and I feel that the radiation has taken its toll on me. But, more importantly, I am hoping it is fulfilling its purpose of killing off my cancer.

As the treatments wind down, I am nearing a total of 36 times in the radiation machine and that's the limit of what I can take. No matter what, I guess, I am through with radiation forever.

February 7, 2013. The 36th and final treatment takes place rather unceremoniously on February 7th. AJ and Janice present me my plastic head-face-neck-chest mask as a keepsake. I am kinda proud carrying it through the waiting room, and I am holding it out in plain sight for everyone to see, but it is obvious they don't give a damn. I walk on to the car with Mary, still a little pissed off from being ignored, and I heave the mask into the back seat. It would have been a great Halloween costume next October, I think, but Mary has other plans: in a couple of weeks she puts it in the dumpster and doesn't even tell me. My Halloween costume is shot down.

The cancer treatments are over but my scheduled visits to most of my doctors continue. I see Doctor Aime Serna, Doctor Bright, and both oncologists several times. All of us are looking forward to May 7th when a PET scan will tell us whether the cancer is gone. Or not.

I have an appointment with Doctor Aime, and Mary leads me and my walker through the parking lot to her office. We walk between parked cars to a raised sidewalk. Mary lifts the front of the walker wanting to help me, but I go off balance and fall backwards. Luckily, I miss hitting the parked cars on my way down, but I hit the pavement with my butt and head at the same time. I am slow to get up, but I keep saying "I'm okay, I'm okay".

I am not okay. A patient in the waiting room sees what has happened, calls for the nurse, and they both rush outside to tend to me. Within a few minutes, they lead me into an examining room, and Doctor Aime takes over. I am mostly shaken up, but there is a small abrasion on the back of my head which she treats. She sees how unstable and weak I am from all the radiation. She contacts Tender Care Home Health, a company with nurses and all kinds of therapists who provide in-home care for recovering cancer patients. My new nurse is Irene Rodriquez who makes a house call to meet me and to determine which therapists will help her with my recovery.

* * *

My Church Pitches In

I attend St. Clement's Anglican Church when I feel strong enough. I sit with friends near the back---where else? Mary sings and sits with the choir upfront. Rev. Bill Francis is our associate minister, and we have developed a close relationship even though I have been a newcomer to the congregation since about a year before I developed cancer. He inquires about my health before services begin on Sunday morning, brings communion to me at home every week or so, and calls me on the phone regularly for any health updates. But he is a busy guy and believes another church member should also visit me at home. This is what the Anglican Church calls a Stephen's Ministry, and its goal is for a layman to establish an ongoing conversation with a recovering patient and provide spiritual guidance as needed. Reverend Francis knows just the guy he wants to assign to me.

Bruce Meyer is very active in the church. He has served in many capacities as a layman: heading up committees, attending various group sessions during the week, and serving on the church board. Bruce and his wife Margaret attend services on either Saturday evening or Sunday early morning. Bruce is in his early 60s and has only recently retired from El Paso's largest insurance company where he was a commercial property salesman and a partner in ownership. And, he is a scratch golfer---one of El Paso's very best.

Like me, he is a member of the El Paso Country Club, but I have never played with him, or even knew him, but I knew of his golfing reputation. After accepting Reverend Francis' assignment as a Stephen's minister to me, Bruce checked around, and found out that I had once been a champion golfer myself (but that was years ago!) This common interest probably led to his assignment to me, and Reverend Francis introduces us to begin the ministry.

Bruce and I agree that every Thursday at 9:30 a.m. will be a good time for us to meet. Mostly, we shoot the bull about golf and UTEP basketball---we are both big fans---and talk a little about politics and the sorry state of affairs in our country. He drinks a large glass of ice tea while I swallow another IsoSource or Ensure Plus.

As our meetings wind up, we join hands and Bruce says a prayer, asking for continued improvement to my health and personal guidance from our God. He leaves me with an upbeat feeling every time he visits. It only takes a few visits before we get to know about each other's families and what we have done with our lives in the past.

That first meeting with Bruce occurred soon after my radiation treatments ended in February 2013, and continues as of this writing. He has become the best non-family friend I ever had---not only through conversation and prayers, but as a care-giver as well. Every week, he peps me up, trying to keep me positive. He has taken me for rides in his Jeep to places I've never been, such as to a mesa in nearby New Mexico for an awesome view of the Franklin Mountains that divide El Paso and separate the United States from another range of huge mountains beyond Juarez in Mexico---that's how El Paso got its name: The Pass. Knowing that I haven't been on the country club golf course for a long while, he has driven me around the 18 holes so that I can see all the improvements that have been made. As a member of the club's board of directors, he is proud of the changes.

From the beginning, Bruce has asked my opinion to solve problems he has incurred from time to time with his golf game. He respects my ability to make good suggestions, primarily about his putting. We work out problems with stance and ball placement on my backyard putting green. He says his putting has improved, but he is using another putter. I hope I helped.

His ministry and friendship are very rewarding to me, and I have expressed my appreciation to Reverend Francis for the relationship he started. It has helped my recovery.

Chapter Four

MY RECOVERY GETS UNDERWAY

ON MARCH 28, 2013, Tender Care Home Health springs into action. Nurse Irene Rodriquez explains that she will visit me twice a week at first, check my blood pressure, and listen to my heart and my lungs. She has scheduled Mario Gardea as my physical therapist, Diana Jaramillo as my occupational therapist, and Denise Salazar as my speech therapist. They are scheduled for treatments in their specialty at least once a week. I trust they all know they have a very weak, physically unstable patient to treat.

* * *

Another Accidental Fall

The fall in front of Doctor Aime's office was not the only time I took a tumble. I fell over one time in the shower and fortunately was only bumped around. No injuries that time. For sure, though, it made me very aware that I can go down without notice, and when I least expect it. Another time, needing to get to my bathroom because of diarrhea, I stagger down the hallway and the next thing I know I fall, and I am on the floor tile. My diarrhea explodes everywhere. It is a huge mess. My daughter-in-law Liliana and my nurse Irene are both nearby, and help Mary get me up, check for any injuries, and clean up the awful mess. My humiliating mistake . . . no walker, no cane, just stupidity. No falls since then.

* * *

Mario is primarily concerned with my balance. He has several items on his agenda. He stands me up straight, has me look straight ahead, and then he walks behind me. Suddenly he gives me a little shove to see if I can regain my balance on my own. Mario is a large man, and he is prepared to catch me if I go down, but I don't even stumble. He works with me on my weight machine, concentrating on my arms and back to see what strength I still have. His workout lasts about an hour. I like him.

Diana is an occupational therapist. Her plan is primarily an exercise routine. I sit in a chair to perform most of her exercises, and sometimes we use a stretchable belt-like strap. Her routine zeroes in on my legs and arms. I find I am getting faster and stronger with each treatment Diana gives me. She is very affable, a good conversationalist. She likes to hike and do every outdoor activity she knows about. She encourages me to do the exercises on my own between her visits.

Denise is the speech therapist. She has a printed page listing each of about ten steps that she tells me to follow when she is there and every day between her visits. I make guttural sounds that are designed to make me use my throat which has been basically inactive since the radiation began months ago. Denise is very pleasant but insistent about my speech exercises, and urges me on. I suspect she knows that my voice and speech may change as time moves along. And she is correct; they do.

Nurse Irene is a textbook care-giver. She does her checking of my vitals promptly and professionally, and always asks about my strength and stability. She wants to know about the therapists' treatments and how they are performing. She always refers to the Tender Care sign-in sheet to verify the consistency and length of visits of each therapist.

If Irene has her way, I will soon be as fit as a 20-year-old athlete, and will be able to speak like a preacher or a politician. She is like a lifelong friend.

* * *

Home Health Care Helps

The home health care program lasts three months, and can be renewed if necessary. Any extension must be approved by the home care nurse and the referring physician. In my case, both agree I am improving, but still need more therapy. When you are housebound, as I am, you appreciate seeing the nurse and therapists, and look forward to their various routines because the treatments seem to be working. So, I am glad when another three months of home care is approved. We don't miss a beat; we continue as before. This second series ends on September 23, 2013. It has been a year since I went to Doctor Morton about that lump in my neck.

* * *

May 7, 2013. The big day finally arrives. The PET scan has been scheduled and, like the two previous episodes before, it is to be taken at the Texas Oncology building on the east side of town. The first, of course, was to determine if I had cancer, and the second a few months later to see if the cancer had spread (it was ordered by Doctor Valilis because I had developed lymphedema in my right hand and forearm, which is a swelling). The swelling remains for a couple of weeks, but my therapist Mario massages it, leads me in hand exercises, and the swelling disappears.

But this PET scan is the one that really counts. The technician, Diana Clement, checks my vitals, pours me a glass of a liquid that I need so that the scan can work the way it is designed. She escorts me to the quiet room where I rest for 45 minutes for the fluid to work its way through my body, and then she leads me to another big machine. She fastens my head in place so it can't move, and wraps a blanket round me so that my arms are stationary. Then the 40-minute scan begins, I don't cough this time, and soon it is over. She tells me the disc and radiologist's report will be forwarded on to Doctors Gupta and Valilis.

May 8, 2013. I am dehydrated and go to the chemo area for an IV drip of the saline solution. No result from the PET scan yet.

May 13, 2013. I meet with Doctor Gupta to hear the verdict. It is good news. No, it is great news! I am free of cancer. None---not even a hint---and I am thrilled to the highest degree. Doctor Gupta says she has no caveats about the result. She leaves her usual business-like manner, breaks into a huge smile, and is as happy as Mary and me. It was an appropriate time for a leaping, chest-bumping high-five!

(Okay, so you don't "chest-bump" with your wife. Or your doctor.)

But the business-like manner returns, and she reminds me that my cancer is in remission. She says it can return at most anytime, but within the next five years is the usual time frame if it is to reappear. Doctor Gupta schedules my next appointment for August 16th.

Doctor Valilis is equally thrilled with the PET scan results. He sets my next appointment for September 9th.

May 31, 2013. Doctor Bright wants to see me at least once a month, unless I have any unforeseen problems. He has seen the PET scan results, and offers his congratulations.

I continue to have the IsoSource pumped through the tube into my stomach. After all these months, it is getting a little bland and I want something else that will give me about the same number of calories. Nurse Irene suggests I try Ensure Plus which contains 350 calories and is available in different flavors. It goes into my stomach through the tube same as the IsoSource, but I imagine I am tasting the butter pecan, the strawberry, and the chocolate flavors of Ensure.

Mary's and my feeding routine continues. Mary is insistent that I should try to eat something a little more solid than the liquids. She keeps harping at me about it, but I keep remembering that months ago I could not swallow when I tried a tamale and some bread products. They seem to collect in my mouth, and just stay there. Even though Doctor Jabalie had fitted and ordered an upper partial plate to replace the teeth he had removed, I cannot chew and I cannot swallow. I occasionally eat a little serving of pudding or Jell-O, but it is more to please Mary than to change from the liquids. I may have a mental block against chewing and eating, but it is real to me, not hypothetical.

* * *

Goodbye to the Stomach Tube

It is now mid-November 2013, and I am sick of the stomach tube and the pumping of the liquids into my stomach. Mary gets an appointment with Doctor Kolli to remove the tube. After what seems like a lifetime in his waiting room, I am finally called into an exam room. He removes some tape around the opening to my stomach, applies an ointment around the tube and then, without warning, he jerks the tube out. I jump about two feet off the table, but it is out after one full year. By the way, I now have two belly-buttons.

* * *

Without the stomach tube, I am no longer eligible for IsoSource paid for by Medicare and I am drinking Ensure Plus instead. Mary and I settle for a drink three times a day consisting of two Ensure Plus and two scoops of ice cream with a scoop of powdered whey protein to beef up the calorie count. At last, the flavor and taste mean something. We are able to get the butter pecan, the strawberry, and chocolate Ensure. We switch around, but the butter pecan is best.

This one drink fills up two glasses: one large and another smaller one to hold the remainder. It is easier for me to drink it through a straw. I am swallowing nearly 3000 calories so I am getting sufficient nutrition and am keeping my weight at about 163 pounds—some 30 pounds less than a year ago. Practically none of my clothes fit any longer, so I spend some time at a nearby alteration shop, and shopping for a new suit. Mary thinks I look like a skinny ghost, but I feel great at this lower weight. I may not look like Nurse Irene's mythical 20-year-old stud athlete, but I think I look pretty good for an old geezer in his mid-80s.

Even though the cancer diagnosis, preparation, and treatment steps are fairly well over, the recovery period continues. Virtually all my doctors want to continue seeing me, although on a less frequent basis. At the August appointment with Doctor Gupta, she says that Doctor Bright is now my cancer doctor, along with Doctor Valilis. She schedules me for January 12, 2015.

At my earlier scheduled August 12th appointment, I don't see Doctor Valilis, but instead I see his assistant, Jennifer Armendariz, an attractive young physician's assistant. It is basically another routine visit, and she schedules my next appointment with their office for December 9th.

My quarterly appointments with Doctor Aime continue. As my primary care physician, she knows all about the cancer result because the other doctors have kept her in the loop.

* * *

A New Radiation Treatment

Reverend Francis telephones to tell me about one of our parishioners, Rob Hoover. Rob has been informed that he has cancer in his throat, just like mine. Reverend Francis says Rob has a lot of questions, and asks me to talk to him. The same day I talked with Rob I read in Texas Monthly *magazine about a new radiation treatment developed at MD Anderson Cancer Center in Houston. It is called "Proton."*

I go through my cancer story with Rob, step-by-step, and I suggest he get a copy of the magazine and read about this new treatment. Rob appreciates the suggestion, visits the Houston center within a few days, is examined, receives all the scan tests, and begins the new treatment.

Rob and his wife travel between Houston and El Paso for a period of about six weeks as he receives the radiation. And then, the Sunday after his treatment cycle ended, I see him at church and we give one another a "man's hug." He has a red area on the front of his neck under his chin that appears to have been caused by a burn from the radiation. He has lost his voice, but his doctors tell him it is only temporary and he would be talking normally again shortly.

And, sure enough, in a couple of weeks his voice comes back, the red area disappears, and he is regaining his strength. As opposed to my experience, he had no dental work, and he had no stomach tube. There is no doubt in my mind that this new treatment is the way to go if one develops throat cancer. You wouldn't know Rob ever had the dreaded disease.

PART TWO

IS IT BELL'S PALSY?

THE MYSTERY DISEASE
YOU DON'T WANT

Chapter Five

NEW PROBLEMS APPEAR

FROM WHAT I HAVE heard, there are many kinds of cancer, and cancer can attack any part of your body. I have had three experiences with cancer, and all three have been located in my mouth or throat. I mentioned earlier about the two sublingual masses that were discovered under my tongue which I had to have removed. In both cases---the first in 1985 and the second in 1992---biopsies were sent to MD Anderson Cancer Center in Houston and to one of those big cancer clinics on the East coast. The pathology report on the first read that the mass was cancer, but that it had been "cured surgically " which means the surgeon got it all. But it was a different story with the second: that report read that "fingerlings" of the mass still remained.

My surgeon at that time, Doctor Pate, gave me my options: 1) do nothing and see what happens, or 2) have surgery to remove all my lymph glands, which means that a surgeon would make an incision from ear to ear just under my chin to remove the lymph glands.

One of the guys I played golf with in Horseshoe Bay in Central Texas had the ear-to-ear surgery several years before, and when I talked to him about it, his recommendation was to do nothing. He had ended up with a dry mouth because his saliva glands had been affected by the surgery, and it was hard dealing with the dry mouth. That sounded like good advice, so I informed Doctor Pate that it was my decision to do nothing.

It did not return, and I never saw Doctor Pate again.

In the recent years since then, I have been to my dermatologist, Dr. Adrian Guevara, a couple of times to treat a rash. He took care of those problems, and I had no further problems. Until:

July 16, 2013. I have an appointment with Doctor Guevara because I notice a red spot on my right cheek and it raises a concern. After his examination is completed, he tells me it is a cancer and that he needs to remove it now. It can be excised in his office, he says, and it won't take long. I tell him to proceed. He makes a vertical incision about two inches long, removes the cancer, and sews my cheek up with 21 stitches. He sets an appointment for two weeks which gives him time to obtain a biopsy report on the cancer he removed. The pathologist's report shows that he has removed a squamous cell carcinoma--- the same kind of cancer I am still recovering from. Doctor Guevara's needlework is flawless. I have no scar.

Then, several weeks later, another red spot shows up in the same location on my left cheek, and I am back in his office. Same story: same in-office surgery, same incision, and the same 21 stitches. Only difference: this time it is a basal cell carcinoma, but the end result is the same: cancer gone, and no scar.

"What a hell of a way to spend two months of my recovery time," I think.

* * *

Time for New Eyeglasses

It is time to have my eyes checked. I make an appointment with my ophthalmologist, Dr. David Schecter, who has written me prescriptions for new glasses several times during the past ten years. I take the prescription to Sam's optical shop to fill, and I order a few extras: transition lenses that change to sunglasses when outside, progressive lenses that eliminate the lines on glasses because I need trifocals, and I select rimless frames because they are . . . well, cool. Five hundred bucks. I pick them up a week later, put them on, the technician adjusts the frames to fit properly, but the lenses are not right. My vision is no better. It seems worse. I tell the technician that I will wear them for a few days and maybe I'll get used to them. I don't. I wonder if the prescription was improperly filled. I go back to Doctor Schecter's office and have the new glasses checked to see if they are what he prescribed. They are. I ask to see the doctor and, when I finally get into his exam room, I tell him something is wrong. He checks my eyes again, writes a new prescription that is totally different than the first one.

The optical shop technician says she will send them back to their shop and have them changed. No charge---it is still under warranty and a remake is free. Again, a week later I pick them up---and they are wrong again. No more Doctor Schecter for me. I go back to the same offices, but this time I see his partner, Dr. Daniel Blumenfeld.

He is much younger than his partner, and he makes no comment about the two mistakes. He begins his own examination. He seems very thorough.

* * *

December 12, 2013. As Doctor Blumenfeld winds up the eye exam, he moves a magnifying instrument close to my left eye. He studies it for several minutes. Then he tells me that he will make an appointment with another eye doctor who also does surgeries that other El Paso ophthalmologists are not qualified to do. He says it is better that he sets up the visit because he can get me in to see the new guy much quicker than I can because he is always very busy.

I am a little confused, and Doctor Blumenfeld senses it.

He says, very casually and briefly, "I want you to be checked for Bell's Palsy".

He makes the appointment for a month away. I take the newest prescription back to the optical shop. The same technician takes the order, looks at my new rimless frames, says the earpiece is broken and has to be replaced. She adds that the frames are under warranty and the shop will replace the frames and fill the new prescription. Again, no charge. I pick up the new glasses a week later.

December 13, 2013. I google Bell's Palsy on my computer to find out what it is so I can understand why I'm scheduled to see the eye surgeon Doctor Blumenfeld has recommended. I find out that the disease is caused when a nerve located behind each ear is damaged. The nerve has three "arms." One leads to your forehead, another to your upper face opposite your ear, and another to your cheek, and each arm has several branches.

I am on the *WebMD* website and I read on:

"The arms control the facial muscles, and when the nerve quits working, the muscles quit working, and the skin on that side of your face begins to sag all the way from your forehead down to your chin."

That is not exactly how the *WebMD* definition reads, but that is what it really says in layman's terms. So far, I do not see any sagging, but I later find out that Doctor Blumenfeld---when he put the magnifying instrument up to my left eye---detected that my lower eye lid was drooping a little bit, and that is why he got the appointment for me with the new eye surgeon.

I am told there is no proven treatment for Bell's Palsy. Nobody seems to know much about it. It is a mystery disease. I find nothing about any treatment, proven or otherwise. There are comments about it vanishing after a couple of months. At least, in most cases.

It seems like time is important. I am hoping that the new doctor knows his business.

January 13, 2014. I am in the office of Dr. Silus Motamarry, the eye surgeon Doctor Blumenfeld mentioned. Doctor Motamarry is a young man, obviously of Indian descent, and he speaks English perfectly. I tell him about the mistakes with the eyeglasses. He checks my vision using the wall charts with the different size letters. He looks into my eyes, but especially the left one. He says nothing about Bell's Palsy and, instead, instructs me to start using an eye drop several times during the day, and an ointment on my eye at bedtime. He schedules my next appointment for April 7th, some nine weeks away.

January 20, 2014. It is time for my regular appointment with Doctor Bright, and my left bottom eyelid is sagging. It is red. Tears cannot flow to my tear duct because the bottom lid is too low causing the tears to puddle. I bring Doctor Bright up-to-date on the glasses debacle and the recommendations of drops and ointment by Doctor Motamarry. He closely examines the eye and suggests he raise the bottom lid by stitching it back to its normal position. He says the stitch is temporary, but it should last until my appointment with Doctor Motamarry in early April. He tapes a weight onto my upper lid to help close the distance between the two lids. After he finishes both procedures, the tears resume their normal flow to the eye duct.

Author John Welsh writes ". . . baby carriages are about the size of a Volkswagen beetle, and block the narrow aisles in medical waiting rooms," and adds the carriages "usually contain enough baby blankets to heat Antarctica."

Doctor Bright schedules the next few monthly appointments because he needs to check on my cancer recovery. During some visits he scopes my throat, and also verifies that the eye stitch is intact. I tell him I will keep him in the loop with any plans made by Doctor Motamarry. Doctor Bright replaces the taped-on weight with a heavier one.

April 7, 2014. Doctor Motamarry examines my eye. He says that the temporary stitch raising the lower lid has collapsed. He wants me to continue with the drops and ointments and wants to see me again on April 29th. He acknowledges that I do have Bell's Palsy, but he has no advice for me. He does not mention any treatment beyond the eye drops and ointment.

April 29, 2014. Doctor Motamarry says it is time for surgery during which he will implant a gold weight inside my upper lid to bring it down and closer to the bottom lid, and will also re-stitch and raise the bottom lid. He wants to see me again on May 16th for pre-op instructions. It has been 19 weeks since Doctor Blumenfeld first brought up Bell's Palsy. I wonder if time for it to vanish is running out.

May 20, 2014. The operation is scheduled at a nearby out-patient surgery center. After the usual interminable delay in the waiting room, I am led to a cubicle and given another hospital gown. Then, I am rolled into the operating room on my bed, and an anesthesiologist immediately injects a liquid into my arm. After a short delay to allow the anesthesia to take effect, Doctor Motamarry begins the surgery. I am in a twilight zone somewhere, but I can hear the conversations between the doctors and nurses. It lasts about an hour, I am rolled back to a recovery area and, after another hour, I am discharged. No pain.

May 28, 2014. Doctor Motamarry checks my eye on May 28th and again on July 8th. He seems to be satisfied with the surgery, but I sense no improvement. My bottom lid sags again, and the upper lid is further away than before. My eye is red again, and the tears are back dripping onto my face. But now, the Bell's Palsy is showing its ugly face. Literally. The left side of my face has also sagged. Big time. The eye brow has slipped off my forehead and onto the space near where my upper lid used to be. Facial skin from my forehead and cheek has slipped, and gravity has created a large gathering near my neck. My lips are crooked, and my mouth slopes downward on the left side. I have no feeling on the left side from my forehead on down. Part of my lips feel dead and the other part is normal. It is almost like there is a wall dividing my face in half. My left nostril is smaller, the right one larger. My left gum inside my mouth feels dead. Unless I pinch my lips together, I drool down a "mini-arroyo," and it flows down and under my chin. I constantly wipe it dry.

I am unhappy with the surgery in May. I can't argue with Doctor Blumenfeld's regard for Doctor Motamarry's abilities, but I believe he missed the mark with me. I cancel my August appointment. He has not helped me at all.

I am ugly. I am sure I will scare kids if they see my face. Boy, what a scary freak I will be on Halloween. I wish I had my radiation mask back.

Chapter Six

A TREATMENT POPS UP

I HAVE MY REGULAR quarterly appointment with Doctor Valilis on August 12th. He has turned me over to his assistant, Jennifer Armendariz. She checks me over, and we talk about my Bell's Palsy. She asks where I am receiving any treatment for it, and I answer I'm not. She looks startled. She has some experience with palsy patients, and says they had recovered after treatment.

She makes an appointment with a therapist at a clinic named Spine & Rehab Specialists for August 22nd. I ask her to refer me also to a neurologist, a specialist dealing with nerves. She has Dr. Jose Lujan schedule me for September 22nd.

She is concerned that I have had the disease for so long. She repeats what I had read on *WebMD* that Bell's Palsy usually disappears within two months or so.

* * *

No One Recommended a Treatment

I leave her exam room and I am angry. I say to myself (and blow my top about it as Mary drives home):

"Why . . . why didn't someone---a doctor or specialist or anybody---tell me to get treatment immediately? None of them said a word to me about any treatment that was available."

I now understand that treatment must come quickly after it begins if treatment is going to help. If you get no treatment and, if it doesn't go away on its own as WebMD *believes it usually does, you are probably going to be stuck with it . . . and its ramifications . . . from now on.*

* * *

August 22, 2014. I am in the registration room at the Spine & Rehab Specialists clinic. When the paperwork is completed, I am turned over to Nancy Silva, a Texas Tech-trained physical therapist. She asks a few general health questions, but zeroes in on my Bell's Palsy.

"When did this begin?" she asks.

I answer, "In January."

"That is a long time ago for this," she responds. "Usually it disappears within a few months, so it is questionable whether it can be reversed after seven months, but we can go through one treatment to see if I sense any facial muscular movement at all."

I tell her I have an appointment with a neurologist on September 22nd, and that I agree that we try at least one treatment. She gets me comfortable on a bed, and explains that she will be administering electrical stimulation. She shows me this instrument (it resembles a small pistol), and says there are six key spots on the left side of my face that she will be aiming the minor electrical voltage at, and she tells me to hold a small unit, which I assume is a part of the "electric gun." After I grasp onto it, she literally pulls the trigger and I feel a little shock. She "fires" a few more shots, then goes to the next location. She asks if I can take the amount of "shock" she is "shooting," and I say it is okay. She moves on to the other locations on my face, and then repeats the treatment two more times. I am aware of the electricity entering my face, but it is painless. The procedure lasts about 20 minutes.

When Nancy finishes, she helps me sit up on the side of the bed while I regain my balance. She says she did feel a slight---very slight---movement, and that she is not sure it will increase with more treatments. I respond that I think it is worth continuing, and she then suggests the stimulation three times a week.

I go to her clinic regularly for a couple of weeks, but the movement is still minor. She wants to continue until my appointment with the neurologist, Dr. Jose Lujan. I tell her I will report back to her what Doctor Lujan plans and what his diagnosis is.

September 22, 2014. Doctor Lujan is a dapper-looking physician, well-trimmed moustache sort of like Cesar Romero, the romantic movie star from the recent past. Doctor Lujan and his staff are friendly and prompt. The staff completes the paperwork and takes all the usual pre-exam tests: blood pressure, weight, height, etc.

We discuss my recent medical episodes, back far enough to cover the cancer diagnosis and the treatment that followed. As we talk, he studies my face and remarks that he doesn't think I have Bell's Palsy! He believes I have a nerve paralysis because the sagging and lack of feeling has been so slow in developing. He repeats (I've heard and read this umpteen times) that Bell's Palsy develops quickly, and usually goes away in a short period of time. He says nothing---one way or the other---about the electrical stimulation.

He schedules me for an MRI at the same Diagnostic Out-patient Imaging Clinic where I was tested earlier. The MRI is set for September 24th and he will know the results next week. The MRI will produce pictures of my brain and my face. *Is he wondering if I had a stroke?*

September 29, 2014. Doctor Lujan is upset as we begin the appointment. He says the diagnostic clinic didn't follow his orders and the MRI recorded my brain, but only a portion of my face. He says he wants another MRI, calls the clinic for an immediate re-do, and sends us back for another test. As Mary and I start to leave, he remarks that there is no problem with my brain, and everything is fine with that part of my head. Mary rolls her eyes.

*   *   *

<u>*Something New? Not Again!*</u>

After the second MRI, I wait at the clinic for the nurse to give me discs of both the first and the second MRI. One of the nurses brings me Doctor Boushka's readings of the treatment just completed. Doctor Bouska finds irregularities with both my thyroid and my right carotid artery. He recommends to Doctor Lujan that I have a CT scan to get a better reading on my neck.

After Doctor Boushka reads the results of the CT scan, he schedules an ultrasound test on both my thyroid and right carotid artery for October 16th. At this point I wonder whether there is some "make work" going on here, because one test seems to discover another potential problem, and that leads to another test, and it goes on and on . . .

The thyroid ultrasound reveals a small nodule and several cysts, and an appointment is scheduled with a thyroid specialist for October 29th. I set up an appointment with my cardiologist, Dr. Ben Matthew, before the thyroid appointment because the ultrasound on my neck showed a "60 to 70 percent stenosis" (which means blockage), and that worries me a lot.

Doctor Lujan's comment that he doesn't know whether I have Bell's Palsy or nerve paralysis, also worries me.

But, it really doesn't matter, does it? I ask myself.

*   *   *

October 20, 2014. Today is a double-header of doctor appointments: Doctor Bright in the morning, and Doctor Matthew in the afternoon.

On my last visit to Doctor Bright in August, he suggested that he can correct the eyelid problem and align my left eyelids with my right side eye, that he can remove the surplus skin on the left side of my face, and that he can level out my sagging mouth---all of this in a three-hour surgery. I told him then that I would consider it, but will wait to see what the electrical treatments at the rehab and the appointment with the neurologist produce. As I thought about the surgery proposal,

I told Mary that if my mouth was leveled I should not drool and I might be able to begin eating solid food again---after two years. We'll see.

But now, though, I know that the electrical stimulation is not going to improve things and that Doctor Lujan does not want to try "nerve conduction," a treatment that Nancy Silva asked him to do in both her e-mails and phone calls. Doctor Lujan, instead of trying the nerve conduction treatment, suggests I have more electrical stimulation. So much for the electrical treatments---I tell Doctor Bright to schedule the surgery.

That afternoon I bring Doctor Matthew up-to-date and tell him about the surgery being scheduled. Immediately, he says he needs to be certain that I . . . being 85 years old . . . can withstand Doctor Bright's three-hour, complex surgery. Before signing off with his approval for the operation, he wants a chemical stress test and another ultrasound by his own technician because he doesn't have confidence in the earlier one. He schedules both tests and sets up a follow-up appointment for November 6th.

October 30, 2014. The chemical stress test is what it sounds like: no treadmill, no exertion of any kind. I am on a bed, and a nurse injects some medicine into a vein. This medicine works its way through my system and provides Doctor Matthew with a picture of my veins and arteries and, most importantly, a good view of my heart. It is a three-hour plus assessment. The ultrasound, originally scheduled for November 17th is switched to tomorrow. I really appreciate the change because it moves us closer to Doctor Bright's planned surgery.

October 31, 2014. It is Halloween, and most of the Heart Center staff leaves in early afternoon. The ultrasound is set for 3:45 p.m., and everything goes off on time. The technician leads me in a small exam room, has me lie down on the bed, and preps me for the test. It takes about 15 minutes. He warns me about getting off the bed too fast and, while I am still sitting on the edge of the bed, I want to know about the result. So, I ask:

"How was the blockage? Was it in the 60 to 70 percent range like my previous test?"
He quickly responds. "No. I don't consider anything less than 50 percent as stenosis.
You're good to go . . . both right and left carotids. I checked them both."
That is good news. I just have to wait until Thursday next week when Doctor Matthew gives me the results and his "yes or no" about the surgery.

*   *   *

An Operation to Check My Blood Flow

My appointment is running late, but after 30 minutes or so the nurse leads me to one of Doctor Matthew's exam rooms. Another 20 minutes pass before the doctor enters.

He says he is concerned about my heart. He says the bottom of my heart is not receiving blood and Mary moves to a large chart on the wall which shows the typical blood flow. She understands what Doctor Matthew is telling us because she spent much of her nursing career as a nurse in heart catheterization surgeries. She points to the general location where the doctor is concerned about. He agrees and points out that the right coronary artery outside my heart may be blocked. He says the only way to know is for me to undergo a heart catheterization (heart cath) operation. I agree, and he orders it to be scheduled at Providence Medical Center across the street from his office.

He explains the procedure. He will insert a long catheter into an artery at my right wrist, and push the catheter through the artery up my arm. He will stop pushing when the catheter reaches the top of my heart. He will be watching on a monitor and, when the catheter is at the place where he will begin his search, he will inject the contrast at my wrist. It will show him where the blockage is located. Depending on what he observes, he may place a stent at the blockage to allow the blood to flow freely.

This sounds like a classroom lecture in Blood Flow 101 at medical school, but I believe I understand. I am also certain Mary will explain it to me later. The heart cath is scheduled for 7:30 a.m. on Monday, November 10th.

* * *

November 6, 2014. When we arrive home, I isolate myself in my office and reflect on my medical issues the past two years. Discovery of the throat cancer, its treatment and recovery, the brief lymphedema episode, and now this Bell's Palsy---if that is what I have---have consumed my older years and have brought a new element into my family's life.

I have prayed to God to please end this medical nightmare, to give me strength to endure what comes, and spare my life for a while longer so that I can see my children and grandchildren grow and develop their lives in a good way---through the tumultuous years of youth and on into the maturity of adulthood. I guess that is what most of us senior citizens want.

Friends remark that they have wondered how I have put up with all these serious events. One of them---feeling philosophical---comments that "you can't grow old if you're a sissy," Another adds, "Or if you're a wimp." They're correct: older folks have to stay strong and must have faith that things will go right. Yes, strong; and brave, too.

Chapter Seven

GETTING PREPARED AGAIN

JOSEPH AND I ARE at Providence Medical Center for the heart cath. I am sent to the out-patient waiting room and soon on to an out-patient cubicle where I change my clothes into another of those see-my-underwear gowns.

Joseph and I talk about his sons and their boarding schools in the Northeast. I see Doctor Matthew in the lab of the out-patient waiting area. My nurse Susan Mantanez preps me for the upcoming operation: I am wired to a telemetry to monitor my heart, and a needle gadget is inserted into my left arm and is connected to a slow-dripping IV bag hanging above my bed. This hook-up also provides a quick entry into my blood system should it be needed in an emergency.

At 9:45 a.m., I am pushed down several corridors atop my hospital bed to the operating room. It is cold. I tell one of the attending nurses that I can't believe they are not working in a parka.

Three different nurses are busy getting everything prepared for Doctor Matthew. An iodine solution is applied to my right wrist and parts of my hand near the location where the catheter will be inserted. One of the nurses tells me to remove my underwear. A sheet covering me from the waist down is removed and more of the iodine solution is applied all around my groin area. Another nurse explains that if a problem arises pushing the catheter through my radial artery, the surgeon will make an opening at the groin and insert the catheter into another artery and push it on to the top of my heart. The surgical nurses are very proficient and patient-friendly.

I notice a track attached to the ceiling. At about that same time, a motor starts up and equipment moves along the track and stops above my upper chest. What I assume to be a monitor is lowered and positioned above my heart facing where Doctor Matthew will stand as he works the catheter to my heart. It is still cold, and nurses place warm blankets over my stomach and legs.

Doctor Matthew begins the procedure. I feel a little activity on the arm which I guess is the catheter being pushed through it; there is no pain. I have received no anesthesia.

And then, within a few minutes, the operation is over---more time was spent getting me prepped than it took for Doctor Matthew to see where the blockage is located. The very small catheter is removed from my arm and wrist, and I am rolled back to my cubicle.

Mary is there and, with the operation over, Joseph leaves. Doctor Matthew tells Mary and me that he did not insert a stent because he felt it was not necessary at this time. He says he will prescribe medication when the upcoming facial surgery is completed. The medicine should improve the blood flow. He repeats that I am an "intermediate risk " (somewhere between low and high risk) for surgery, but that he will contact Doctor Bright about the results of the heart cath and discuss the proposed operation. He tells us to call his office for an appointment Thursday.

Susan, my registered nurse, removes the IV needle from my left arm. She places a small pad of gauze over the small hole under my right wrist, and puts a transparent bandage over the gauze pad and seals its edges to my skin. Then she attaches a cast about nine inches long above my right wrist to help prevent movement.

I had anticipated a cut of some size on my wrist where the catheter is to be inserted, but it is tiny---about one-eighth inch long. No stitches. Only a drop of dried blood shows.

Susan tells me I must not use my right hand for anything: *"Don't bend it, don't lift anything for 24 hours," she tells me.*

She warns that I don't want a hematoma to form under my skin and, if it does, it will resemble a small balloon and I should immediately call 911 and get to the hospital. Later Mary explains to me that a hematoma is a massive clot of blood under the skin and any activity of my wrist can cause it to gather. It is blood that has leaked from the artery. I remove the gown and put on my own clothes. We drive home.

* * *

Intermediate Risk for Surgery

It is Thursday following the heart cath, and Doctor Matthew is prepared to go over the results. He says he saw a lesion (injury) on one of the arteries, but then his description of the procedure is mostly medical terms. He mentions disease, dampening, hemodynamics, gradient---all medical words that I don't understand. He says there were no complications and, when he completed the operation, I was stable and free of any chest pain.

He calls Doctor Bright, discusses the procedure, and tells him his findings of the heart cath. More medical terms. He says again that I am an intermediate risk for the pending surgery.

I get a copy of his two-page report as we leave. As soon as Mary and I arrive home, I fax copies to both Doctor Bright and Doctor Aime Serna. I ask for appointments to discuss the facial surgery. Doctor Bright is booked solid until December 5th and I hope to get in to see Doctor Aime within the next few days.

I admit to myself that I am "waffling" on proceeding with the complex surgery proposed by Doctor Bright. I am concerned about the intermediate risk comments by Doctor Matthew, the unexplained lesion he found during the heart cath, his decision not to insert a stent at the blockage, and his closing remarks in his report:

"I believe the best course of action for the patient is to continue medical therapy for now. Patient will be started on a low-dose beta-blocker and continue on with surgery."

He says the medicine should improve the blood flow through the artery branches in the lower part of my heart. I am confused about what to do. I go over these doubts with Mary, and she brings up another point. She remembers I had trouble trying to swallow a communion wafer the previous day when Rev. Ron Thomson brought communion to our home.

"What advantage is there for wanting a level mouth if you have problems swallowing?" she asks.

"None," I answer. "I miss eating solid foods, but the drinks go down easily. Maybe I can try harder to chew soft foods, and hold my lips tight while I chew and swallow. That way I won't drool."

Mary adds, "The operation won't bring back the feeling you've lost on your face. You will still have the dead gums and dead tongue. You might consider having Doctor Bright fix just your eyelids---not your face."

I remind her that it was a simple procedure when he stitched up my lower eyelid months ago.

"That was a temporary fix, but maybe he could make it last longer," I respond.

After a little more discussion, I tell Mary I will wait until I have a chance to discuss all of this with the two doctors.

* * *

November 26, 2013. Doctor Aime Serna calls and wants an update on the proposed surgery by Doctor Bright. I thank her for calling, and tell her I need her opinion on the extent of the surgery. We discuss Doctor Matthew's report on the heart cath, and I tell her I am strongly considering having Doctor Bright operate on the eyelids and not the facelift, at least for now. I remind her that she has been my main doctor for many years now, and that I greatly respect her opinion.

Without hesitation, Doctor Aime agrees that I should proceed with eyelid portion of the surgery.

December 5, 2014. My appointment with Doctor Bright begins early, and we immediately discuss the surgery. I explain that the intermediate risk label from Doctor Matthew does cause some apprehension, and that it is more important to me that he stitches up my lower eyelid and add more weight into the upper lid. He agrees that the facelift will not change any of the effects of the palsy. He says the extent of the surgery is my call. I say my main concern is that he fix my eyelids.

Doctor Bright then studies my eye and the lids very carefully, and then says he believes that there will be some levelling of my mouth when he raises the bottom lid. Even a slight amount of raising the left corner of my mouth should stop or greatly reduce the drooling down my chin onto my upper neck. He laughs when I call that my "mini-arroyo."

He explains that I will receive anesthesia for the surgery, and that I will not know what is going on during the operation. He asks that Mary and I stay in his waiting room while he and his staff schedule the surgery. Shortly, his scheduler gives us all the necessary paperwork and prescriptions and informs us that the operation will take place on December 16th at Las Palmas Medical Center. She suggests that I pre-register with the hospital several days before, and says that I will not need any X-rays or blood work since it was done recently by Doctor Matthew.

Mary and I are happy with the schedule. I want to get the lids back to their proper location as soon as possible because the tears and blurry eyesight are getting worse. But, I have complete confidence in Doctor Bright, and respect for his judgment to make correct decisions during the surgery. I believe he will do what is necessary.

* * *

<u>Another Family Medical Issue</u>

Earlier in this narrative I detailed the automobile accident that son Joseph and some of his family experienced in New

Hampshire two-plus years ago. Now another health crisis has developed, and this time it is Joseph who is the victim.

In the past few weeks he has been re-arranging merchandise in one of our markets. This involves a lot of stooping and bending and lifting heavy cases of products. He notices a large lump in his groin area, and another in his neck near his right shoulder. His primary care doctor, Dr. Branch Craige, examines both areas and sends Joseph to Dr. Gerard Crecca, a general surgeon.

Doctor Crecca orders CT scans of both. Several days later, Doctor Crecca and a pathologist inform Joseph that cancerous nodules are throughout his body and that he has non-Hodgkins lymphoma, a dangerous but treatable disease. The CT scans also reveal a hernia, and the doctors recommend immediate surgery to repair the hernia so that he will have some time to recuperate before he begins an intense 18-week long treatment of chemotherapy and supporting drugs. Joseph's hernia surgery on November 25th goes well, and he spends a few days at home recovering.

The chemo will be infused through a porta-catheter placed inside a large vein in his chest, and the chemo and drugs will be administered during an all-day session on Thursdays, three weeks apart. Doctor Crecca warns Joseph that he will feel okay the following day---Friday—but that he will feel awful from the chemo and drugs on Saturday and Sunday following.

"It will be the worst days of your life," he predicts.

This schedule means he will receive six treatments over the 18-week cycle. He will lose his hair, lose some weight, will become anemic, and his immune system will be affected. Doctor Crecca recommends he avoids people as much as possible and, when he is around other people, that he wears a mask covering his nose and mouth to ward off germs.

The process begins on Tuesday, December 9th with a PET scan to better locate the cancerous nodules, then minor surgery to implant the porta-catheter on Wednesday, December 10th, and the first chemo/drug treatment the following day. Odds on destroying the cancerous nodules range from 58% to 80%.

However, things suddenly change. Early on Wednesday, December 10th, in the middle of the night, Joseph suddenly has problems breathing and Liliana drives him back to Providence Medical Center emergency room. The doctors on duty take X-rays and determine the lymph nodules have partially filled his lung, causing the difficulty in breathing. Doctor Crecca examines him the following morning, and calls in a pulmonologist. Medication improves his breathing, and it is decided that he remains in the hospital. Doctor Crecca and Doctor Valilis agree to keep the original schedule, and the porta-catheter is implanted on December 10th. They further decide that the full-day chemo/drug treatment begins in late afternoon the same day, and be completed on Friday, and that it be administered in the hospital instead of at the Texas Oncology Center. He feels fine and is released from the hospital on Saturday.

I am very optimistic for Joseph's full recovery because of what I have learned from my research, plus the fact that his oncologist is Doctor Valilis, the same chemo-oncologist I had when my throat cancer was discovered two years ago.

My personal optimism is somewhat clouded with my personal bewilderment. I find it hard to accept---much less to even understand---why so many bad things are happening in my family: one after another, on and on and on. But, one bright side: growing old does provide one with the experience and confidence that everything will turn out okay.

* * *

December 8, 2014. Doctor Bright calls for me to come into his office so that he can select the correct size of the metal weight he will install inside my upper eyelid during the surgery scheduled for next week. He allows for the weight previously placed there by Doctor Motamarry. After trying several different ones, Doctor Bright arrives at a weight that should provide the correct distance between the upper and lower eyelid.

He says he will likely make at least one incision on my left cheek so that he can move the facial skin enough to allow him to raise the lower lid and, hopefully, raise the left corner of my mouth which should make it easier for me to chew and swallow both liquids and solids. Whatever he can do to get my left eye back close to normal is all right with me. Yes, I would like for my mouth to be corrected, but the eye is most important. The constant flow of tears and the blurred vision I now have is very uncomfortable. I cannot see well. My glasses are very little help, and it is certain I will have to obtain a new prescription after the surgery is completed and my left eye has adjusted to the changes.

* * *

My Face Is Not Pretty

I am not planning on a "before and after" photograph, but I ask Mary to take a photo of my face before the surgery. She takes several with my iPad. And here is what they show:

Yes, I am still ugly. Maybe worse. On the left side of my face, my eyebrow is slightly below my forehead and the brow hairs are growing in all directions. The lower eyelid is sagging a lot and the top side of my lower lid is almost a half-circle. You can see tears that have no place to go until they drip down my cheek. The perimeter of my eye is totally red---completely bloodshot. My nose is neither vertical nor straight, and appears broken. The left corner of my mouth still sags and slopes downward toward my chin. My lips are dry and show cracks. That large gathering of skin that has slipped from my cheek looks like someone chewing tobacco. It doesn't match the right side of my face. Nothing matches the right side of my face. My mini-arroyo that carries liquids from my sloping mouth to my chin is still there, perhaps a little deeper.

All in all, it is not a pretty picture. If, as they say, beauty is only skin deep, I don't know what they would say about this. I doubt it could be worse.

Chapter Eight

THE COMPLEX SURGERY

MY SURGERY IS SCHEDULED for December 16th at 12:30 p.m. at Las Palmas Medical Center. There is a surgery cancellation and the hospital telephones and asks us to check-in at 10:30 a.m., an hour earlier than scheduled. Doctor Bright believes I will have to stay at least one night in the hospital following the surgery.

After checking-in, Mary and I sit in the waiting area for a short while and are soon led to the surgery area and shown into a cubicle. I receive another one of those gowns with the "rear" window, a pair of hospital slipper-socks, and a large draw-string bag to pack my shoes and clothing. My nurse makes sure both Mary and I are comfortable and she hands me a remote to call for help or for turning on the television. And then, the inevitable wait begins. What I believe will become surgery at 11:30 because of the cancellation, turns into a delay. We wait. And we wait some more.

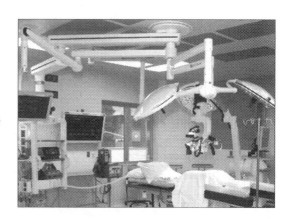

A state-of-the-art operating room at Las Palmas Medical Center in El Paso, TX.

After about three hours, a young lady dressed in surgery scrubs and wearing one of those balloon-like hats they wear in operating rooms, parts the privacy curtains and walks into the cubicle. She introduces herself as Laura Meaney, and advises us that she is my anesthesiologist.

The three of us discuss just about everything but the upcoming operation. And then she asks my nurse to email Doctor Matthew's office across the street to send her the two-page report prepared after my heart cath, some ten days ago. It arrives in a few minutes. She is apparently concerned about the intermediate risk for surgery comment in Doctor Matthew's report.

She leaves for a few minutes, returns, and explains that she will infuse the anesthesia through the same IV needle in my left wrist where I have been receiving an IV drip. She says she will also have an instrument with a camera on the end of it and will insert it down my throat. And then, she pushes the privacy curtains apart, makes certain that the rails on my bed are up and locked in place.

Laura has a helper pushing the back of my bed, and she grabs the front and leads the way. Obviously the wait is over, and we are on our way to the operating room. Finally.

$$* \quad * \quad *$$

Another Operating Room

We pass cubicle after cubicle en route to the surgery area, through two wide automatic doors into another corridor that looks like it is 100 yards deep. There are several male surgery nurses in the corridor which is stocked with pallets of supplies along the walls. Two of the nurses take over my hospital bed and wheel me toward my operating room. It is cold. The nurses are all wearing white sweaters under their scrubs. We pass several other operating rooms. Then, suddenly, we make a right turn into mine.

Another male surgery nurse introduces himself as Oscar and asks if I would like another blanket.

"Please," I answer.

He covers me from my chest down, and he moves me from my hospital bed onto the operating table. Laura walks past the operating table, gives me a thumbs up. I look around for Doctor Bright, but I can't see much. Laura is fiddling with the IV needle on the left wrist . . . and goodnight . . . I enter the twilight zone . . .

* * *

It is after 6 p.m. when I leave the *anesthesia fog.* The surgery is over. The intermediate risk patient has survived. I am tired and numb. I am in a recovery cubicle. Doctor Bright talks to Mary and says everything went as planned. My eye and my cheek are swollen, I am told, but I look very good. Really?

I rest for about an hour and the anesthesia has worn off to the point where I am pushed to my private room on the fifth floor of Las Palmas Medical Center. I am in a very nice room: private bathroom with shower, a television, comfortable chair for a visitor, and a wall loaded with electrical outlets, plugs, wires, lights, telephone, and a rack for the IV and oxygen units. The ever-present IV drip is dripping away. I am sleepy; Mary feels comfortable enough to leave for home.

* * *

The No-Sleep Zone

Sleep---at least for any length of time---is impossible in any hospital, and Las Palmas is no different. During the night, I am awakened so a nurse can take my blood pressure, pulse, and oxygen level. I am awakened so a nurse can insert the oxygen tubes into my nostrils. I am awakened so a nurse can bring me a urinal since it would be risky for me to try to walk to the private bathroom. I am awakened so a nurse can check my vitals. Again. I am awakened so a nurse can give me two pain pills and two antibiotic pills. I am awakened so a nurse can check the oxygen and the IV drip unit. And it is still before midnight. I ask one of the nurses what is the correct time. Oh, I just did that 15 minutes ago. Oh, and then there is the continuous laughter from the several floor nurses who must be at the nurses' station watching a Seinfeld *re-run.*

The rest of the night is about the same. At about 5 a.m. another nurse tells me I will be getting a liquid diet for breakfast (which was actually brought to my bed at about 9:00 a.m.) More checking of my vitals, more pain and antibiotic pills (I have had negligible pain), removal of the oxygen tube from my nose, another urinal, etc. You get the picture---it is a long, long night and any sleep over five minutes is out of the question.

*   *   *

Mary returns at about 7 a.m. and a nurse informs her that Doctor Bright says I can go home when the discharge and paperwork procedures are completed. An hour later, a nurse tells me it will take another hour to prepare the discharge papers which must be signed before I can leave. But the hospital has another tactic to keep you from bolting out the door, escaping down the elevator, and racing through the lobby . . . heading for the parking lot. And that tactic is to keep the IV in place--- dripping away---because it is attached to that IV needle that is securely taped and bandaged to your wrist. You couldn't leave if you had to. Oh well, I can wait those extra 60 minutes for the paperwork to be completed.

A nurse brings me the special liquid diet breakfast: cream of wheat cereal, orange juice, coffee and something else I didn't want anyway. I don't want to eat; I want to leave. My assigned nurse brings in the discharge papers which amounted to about three pieces of paper. Mary signs for me because my handwriting resembles wall graphics in an Egyptian tomb. My nurse removes the IV rig from my wrist, tells me to dress, and that she will return in a few minutes with a wheelchair to take me to the front door where Mary can pick me up.

It is time for another of those high-five chest-bumps, but I can't see Mary because my eye is swollen. I don't steal the gown or the slipper-socks. The wheelchair arrives, and off we go. It is only fair, however, to praise Las Palmas. Every employee I encounter is extremely patient-friendly, thoroughly trained, and available when you need one. It is my first time in the Las Palmas facility and I don't want a second time, but, if I do, Las Palmas will be my choice.

They even have a staff that comes to your home to see how you are doing after you are discharged. And, yes, they have many waiting rooms . . . on every floor.

* * *

Changing Facial Features

I can't help but wonder what I look like after Doctor Bright's "complex" surgery and, the minute I walk into the house, I head for the nearest mirror. I am still ugly, but in a different way. The eye looks great: the bottom lid no longer sags but, instead, it is in the correct position. So is the upper lid. They align almost perfectly with the right eye.

The mouth is completely different that it was before the operation. Now, instead of being sloping diagonally downward toward my left chin, it is sloping upward. My lips do not meet at the left corner of my mouth. One of my teeth still shows slightly when I try to close my lips. Instead of having a perpetual frown, now I have a huge smile. Remember Jack Nicholson as "The Joker" in the Batman movie? That's me. No joke.

Doctor Bright had to make several incisions on the left side of my face. There is one cut about one inch long parallel to my nose and about a quarter of an inch away. There is another one, about the same size between my eye and hairline. He inserted a piece of treated cadaver tissue between these incisions under my skin to help fill in an indention in my cheek below my eye. That area is swollen and puffy. (To put my mind at ease, he says the cadaver tissue has no cells and will not grow or change shape.)

He has made a third incision, horizontal, in my upper eyelid to remove the small weight that Doctor Motamarry inserted in the previous operation, and to install a heavier gold weight in its place to bring it down, nearer the lower lid. A fourth incision, this one vertical, is near the left corner of my mouth. The stitches to close the various incisions look okay, and any scars that remain will be difficult to detect.

My main concern---the droopy left eye with dripping tears ---looks normal. The swelling that occurs after most surgeries is minimal. I feel certain it will disappear within a few days. Actually, I am relieved with the results---at least, so far.

* * *

December 22, 2014. It is the Monday following surgery, and I have an early appointment with Doctor Bright to remove the stitches. He goes into some of the details of the operation, including installation of two small pieces of some metal to hold the cadaver tissue in place. The metal plates are anchored to my skull, and held in place by what Doctor Bright calls "small bolts!"

I am not too thrilled to hear about that.

Doctor Bright suggests I massage the area under my eye where the swelling is the worst. That will help the swelling disappear. He seems satisfied with the results. He says the tilting of my mouth upward at the corner will sag enough so my mouth will become level and that should make it easier to eat and eliminate the drooling. (I hope I can remember how to eat since it has been over two years since I have tried solid foods.) He sets another appointment for the middle of January.

* * *

More Changing Facial Features

It has been about three weeks since Doctor Bright removed all the stitches from the surgery, and I am not certain at this point whether the operation was a success. The eyelids are nearly perfect in lining up with the right eye, and the scars are healing and are almost invisible. I do have a spot on my left cheek that is sunken in and appears like a bruise. What I though was swelling below my eye is a hump from the cadaver tissue that was inserted. But there are a couple of problems. First, my vision is lousy: if I am watching TV, the images are blurry and the tears are not flowing to the tear duct. If I try to close the left eye or put on an eye patch to use only the good eye, it is no better. I wonder whether I will ever see well again, and I fear the lower eyelid needs to be closer to the upper one which could mean another surgery. And I don't want that, but I want to see clearly once again. My next appointment with Doctor Bright is still about ten days away, unless I can get an earlier appointment.

Second, I cannot close my mouth. An opening at the left corner of my mouth---probably caused by the incisions and stitches needed to level my mouth---keeps my lips apart. I have to clamp the lips together with one hand while I hold a glass of Ensure or water in my right hand. Plus, the opening affects the way I use a straw because it is difficult to create sufficient suction to pull the liquid from the glass into my mouth. I hope Doctor Bright's feeling that gravity will close the opening turns out to be an accurate assessment.

I have often heard that those with Irish breeding are pessimistic and negative---a cultural thing. In my case, that could well be correct because, with all the health problems that have come my way since I was first diagnosed with cancer, had I decided to forego the radiation and chemo, it would have worsened by now and I would probably be dead and I would have missed the Bell's Palsy and several surgeries. Yes, that is negative. Or, is it?

* * *

January 12, 2015. My scheduled appointment with Doctor Gupta is today. Her nurse calls, asking for every event that has transpired since I saw Doctor Gupta last August. She wants the details of the MRIs, the CT scans, the ultrasounds, the two surgeries---all of that. The heat cath slips my mind, and I call her back to add to her list. Doctor Gupta quickly reviews all of the procedures that took place since I saw her last. She asks if I am eating solid food yet, and I answer that I am not because I have a problem chewing anything solid, and then swallowing it. She is unhappy with me. I suppose patients with throat cancer have different problems once the radiation is over but I know that . . . no matter how hard I have tried . . . I am unable to chew solid food enough that I can swallow it.

She tells me to see a therapist whom she says will train me to chew and swallow. That suggestion ends our appointment, and I assume Doctor Gupta's nurse will provide me with the information about the therapist.

January 16, 2015. Doctor Bright is concerned about the slow-healing of the incision outside my left eye. It continues to ooze yellow matter. He believes he made the incision where a squamous cell skin cancer was located just below the skin. He cleans the area thoroughly and hopes it will heal up. He suggests I schedule an appointment with Doctor Guevara---my dermatologist---since there are several places on my left cheek that he suspects are skin cancers and need to be removed. The small "hole" outside my mouth is also infected, and Doctor Bright prescribes an antibiotic to clear it up. Both he and I are relatively happy with the surgery outcome---I know my appearance is much better than it was before the operation. Not good, but better.

February 5, 2015. Doctor Guevara wants the details of the recent surgery. He is mainly interested in the incision at the edge of my eye which Doctor Bright feared was made through a squamous cell carcinoma. I tell them that Doctor Bright had a biopsy analyzed, and it is cancer.

Doctor Guevara takes biopsies of the questionable places near my left temple. He will receive the pathologist's report in several days, and will schedule another appointment when he knows the results. Several days later, his office sets me up for another appointment for Tuesday, March 3, 2015, and I am told to be prepared for up to four hours because it appears I will undergo a Moh's Procedure to remove more skin cancer.

February 9, 2015. The speech therapist that Doctor Gupta said would help me learn how to eat again called, and set up an appointment for today. The therapist is Kara Yepo, and her assistant is Selina Salazar.

They have a multi-page list of different exercises that are designed to strengthen my tongue, my lips, and my ability to swallow. The session is fast-moving, and lasts 45 minutes. Throughout the battery of exercises. I am wired up to a machine that is emitting electrical stimulation to my throat. It is very similar to the electrical treatment administered by Nancy Silva when she was attempting to reverse the damage caused by Bell's Palsy. I am scheduled for treatments on Mondays and Wednesdays early afternoon.

As these treatments progress during the next few weeks, I find they are getting easier and easier. Although I continue to have no feeling from the left side of my tongue, I seem to have more movement from my right cheek and the right side of my tongue. Kara and Selina have had me chew gum and eat applesauce as what I consider a preliminary step in teaching me to chew and swallow solid foods. However, this is not easy and it is somewhat messy. When I switch the chewing gum from the right side to the left side of my mouth, the gum slips out through the opening between my lips on the left side of my mouth. I find I can chew gum fine on the right side, and the therapists encourage me to chew gum at home, using only that right side.

The applesauce is a different story. When I take a small amount from a spoon, some of it comes out the opening of my lips. I take a drink of cold water after each couple of bites. I have to wipe off my lips and chin after each bite. But, I sense some progress---and that is what I have been looking for.

* * *

February 23, 2015. I want to see Doctor Bright before the appointment with Doctor Guevara on March 3rd. I want to be sure that the two doctors have had a chance to discuss my facial issues before the Moh's Procedure. I need to be certain myself of the exact location of the two metal plates beneath my left eye because I believe Doctor Guevara will be removing cancers close to the metal plates and the cadaver tissue that the plates are holding in place.

But, my attempt to get an appointment with Doctor Bright is unsuccessful---he is booked solid for several weeks. However, I am able to talk to him on the phone, and he assures me that he has discussed my situation thoroughly with Doctor Guevara, including the location of the metal plates. With that understanding, I plan to proceed with the upcoming appointment with Doctor Guevara.

March 3, 2015. Doctor Guevara deadens the area around the spot where the Moh's Procedure will begin. After he is certain I am numb, he removes the cancerous area, puts it under a microscope and finds it is not cancerous, just an area where stitches were placed by Doctor Bright back in December. The Moh's Procedure is now unnecessary, and Doctor Guevara says my face will be free of skin cancer after he completes a little maintenance work on both sides of my face.

While my left side is still numb, he scrapes away the questionable places, and takes biopsies. Then he freezes about eight spots on my right cheek and upper neck. There are four bright red areas now after the scraping, and Doctor Guevara has these raw areas covered in bandages which I must keep in place for one full day. He wants to see me again in three months at which time he will work on the "dimple," or "hole" outside the left corner of my mouth. Hopefully that will close up the opening there which prevents me from completely closing my lips together.

March 5, 2015. As time moves forward, I may have to see Doctor Guevara again if the usual skin cancers continue to reappear. And, recalling that Doctor Gupta said that Doctor Bright is "now your cancer doctor," I will continue at least an every two-month appointment schedule with Doctor Bright. This will give me the opportunity to have him scope my throat to see whether there is any sign of the cancer returning.

March 23, 2015. Doctor Guevara telephones to inform me that one of the biopsies he took three weeks ago is cancerous and that he will perform a Moh's Procedure tomorrow. I am not certain exactly which of the four spots is the problem.

But before Doctor Guevara works on me, I am worried that it might be very close to where Doctor Bright fastened the metal plates to my skull to hold the cadaver tissue when he operated back in December. I am fortunate that Mary was able to get me an appointment today. Doctor Bright shows me exactly where the metal plate is located, and tells me he has informed Doctor Guevara that it be okay to remove the plate if it interferes with the Moh's Procedure. He agrees that my lower left eyelid has drooped slightly and that tears are puddling there again. He says he will raise it back into its proper place once again, but not until Doctor Guevara has finished on my left cheek. That means another surgery.

March 24, 2015. Doctor Guevara is able to remove the cancerous area next to my left ear. He cuts away an area about the size of a nickel coin. No stitches are needed and, after he examines the skin he removed under his microscope, he finds no more cutting is required because all the cancer is gone. His nurse bandages the area thoroughly and instructs me to leave the bandage in place until after I shower tomorrow, then remove it and keep it covered with Vaseline for several days while it heals. Doctor Guevara will examine me again in early May. As soon as the area heals, I will see Doctor Bright again to raise the eyelid. Could this saga be nearing an end? As always, time will tell.

Vision from my left eye is gradually getting worse, or so it seems. And, it changes from day to day---some days it is better than others. Tears continue to puddle above the lower eyelid. Because things look blurry when this happens, I dab at the puddle with a facial tissue, but that doesn't help for long. I schedule an appointment with Doctor Bright for April 16th. I hope he can do whatever is necessary to help me see correctly again.

April 16, 2015. Doctor Bright has a very busy practice. He performs many tonsillectomy and adenoidectomy surgeries on children Tuesdays through Thursdays---among other operations on adults---and sees patients on Mondays and Fridays. He has a cancellation on Thursday and I am fortunate to get an appointment in the early afternoon.

I worry that he is getting sick and tired of seeing me, but our patient-doctor relationship is fine. He even addresses me as "Johnny" instead of "Mr. Welsh," and that certainly makes me feel that he is doing all he can to help me through the various health issues.

After I explain to him how the tear problem seems to be increasing, he carefully studies the movement on both eyes, has me close and open each one. He studies my mouth, especially the opening on the left corner there I cannot fully close my lips.

He suggests another surgery---this one in a day surgery center. He says it will not take long, probably only 30 minutes, and he will use only "local" anesthesia. He will take permanent stitches on each end of my left eyelids to align them with the right eye. Additionally, he will also take stitches on the left end of my mouth to straighten it horizontally. He will also consider trying to eliminate the "hole" or "dimple" on my cheek near my mouth.

"Let's do it," I answer.

It sounds simple enough, and I will be an out-patient, able to go home after a short recovery period. Doctor Bright's surgery scheduler sets us up for next Thursday, April 23rd.

April 23, 2015. Although I am scheduled to report to El Paso Day Surgery at 11:30 a.m., a nurse calls at 8:45 a.m. and asks if I could get there earlier.

"Sure," I say. "What time instead?

"Well, could you come now?" she asks.

"Yes, ma'am," I respond. "We're on our way."

The day surgery center is a new three-story building convenient to many doctor's offices and Sierra Medical Center. The offices and the operating areas are attractive, decorated with Southwestern art and first-class furnishings. It has two waiting rooms in the check-in area: one for parents and adults, and another next to it for children. Many doctors perform tonsillectomies and adenoidectomies there.

Soon after registering at 9:15 a.m., Mary and I are led to our cubicle. A nurse asks for my health information, provides me with another of those "see my underwear" gowns and slip-proof socks. After I change into the hospital garb, another nurse fastens to my chest about eight or ten patches for the leads to the EKG machine to check my heart beats. Another nurse has the EKG done again for some unknown reason.

A needle gadget is attached to my left arm for the drip solution which contains a "mild" anesthesia which Doctor Bright calls a "margarita." He explains exactly where he will stitch my eye and mouth, and then I am rolled to the operating room. Doctor Bright's team consists of an anesthesiologist and two nurses.

I feel nothing other than when he touches to make the stitches. I am awake, I can hear the crew talking, but I am in a mild "twilight zone"---kinda awake and kinda not. Sure enough, it is all over in 45 minutes, and I am rolled to a recovery cubicle.

Doctor Bright seems happy with the way I look, and reminds us that he will remove the stitches on May 1st, eight days from now.

Mary has a small hand mirror and she hands it to me so I can see what I look like. Ugly. Maybe uglier. An incision through the "hole" in my cheek has eliminated it. There are about ten stitches there. There are several stitches at both corners of my eye, but it is impossible to see clearly because my eye has swollen. I'll probably have a "shiner" tomorrow. Several stitches close an incision at the corner of my mouth and, hopefully that will enable me to completely close my lips.

I am a little shaky. A nurse pushes my wheelchair to the front entrance, helps me into the car. We head home.

Mary guides me into the house while I hold onto her shoulders for stability. She gives me a choice of resting on our bed or on my Lazy Boy recliner in the family room, which I select. I try to watch television, but things are blurry. My untouched right eye is also blurry . . . I fear that the new glasses prescription is not correct and I will have to get new ones again after the effects of the surgery end.

I am already looking forward to the removal of the stitches next week. Each day seems a lifetime. Because of the incisions and stitches at my mouth, I cannot drink through a straw as before since there is some pain when I pinch my lips together to avoid drooling. If I clamp my lips together as I did before the surgery, I do not drool. But now, with those stitches in place, I take only short, small sips of liquids, and it takes more time to drink my Ensure-Ice Cream meals to keep up my calorie count at 2000-plus.

I still dab at the tears in my left eye---very gently. I don't want to alter any of the stitches at the corners of my eye.

*   *   *

A Clean Bill of Health

Our son Joseph is nearing a milestone in his battle with lymphoma. After winding up his tri-weekly doses of chemo and supplemental drugs three weeks ago . . . after an all-revealing PET scan . . . he received the verdict today, May 4th. Once again . . . it is good news---no sign of any cancer, anywhere. The intense chemo, the supplemental drugs, and the Neulasta shot---all in one treatment---have killed all the cancerous nodules from his lymph glands. Now, he can look forward to his and his family's future. The therapy he received is the most "lethal" chemo used today. The doctors and nurses administering the chemo wear hazmat suits for protection. The Neulasta jump-starts the growth of his white blood cells . . . a step necessary for a healthy immune system and bone marrow. Our prayers are answered.

* * *

May 1, 2015. The waiting room at Doctor Bright's office is nearly fully of patients---mostly small children with their parents. After I am called in and my vitals taken, I am led into a "mini-operating room" that contains a chair which is adjustable so that I lie level, making it easier for the doctor to remove the stitches.

Within a few minutes, Doctor Bright has removed them from my lower lip, from the incision near my mouth, and from the corners of my left eye---a little uncomfortable but no pain. The longest incision is a little more than an inch long and required about ten stitches to tighten the skin on my cheek and eliminate the "hole." He pulls out a piece of thread about two inches long. All the others were shorter.

His nurse leads me to a regular exam room, fully equipped for the scope procedure to see whether the mother cancer has returned. I have worried about this because my voice has changed somewhat . . . at least to me. I must speak a little louder and a little slower than before to be understood.

Doctor Bright inserts the scope into my right nostril and eases it down until he can clearly see my throat, my voice box, and the upper portion of my esophagus. The scope's tiny camera records everything, and we watch a replay and Doctor Bright narrates. He says everything is perfectly normal. There are a couple of tiny red spots which he says were left from the radiation and that they are harmless. That is a major relief to me: no return of the cancer and no problem with my voice box. Another high-five, chest-bumping moment.

As he ends the appointment, I thank him for all the *"good work, care and concern that (he) has shown me over these past thirty months."* He appreciates my remarks and winds things up by telling me to get an appointment in six to eight weeks, unless there is need for him to see me before that. Mary, our son Jem (who has accompanied us for this appointment), and I leave.

* * *

This will be My Recovery

As we drive away, I feel a new sense of satisfaction: my cancer is gone (at least for now), my lymphedema is history, and my Bell's Palsy has done its damage which I will live with. My vision is not good: In order for me to be able to close my left eye, Doctor Bright had to compromise during the last surgery. He had to take into account the weight of the gold weight he inserted inside my upper lid. If he stitched it any higher, I would be unable to close my left eye. So I have blurry image with my left eye, and a continuation of tearing. My right eye is fine, but I catch myself closing my left eye and reading or watching television with only my right eye.

I still have some minor obstacles ahead of me, but nothing I can't handle. The loss of feeling with the left side of my tongue has affected my speaking and I am concerned that I am hard to understand; so, I speak slower and more definite. The left side of my face continues to sag, and some skin gathers near my chin. The gap between my lips is better, but not perfect.

I'm not ready for solid foods, I'm not ready for golf again . . . but I am alive and I am not scheduled for anything requiring a waiting room . . . no crying kids, no narrow aisles, no flowery chairs, no Volkswagen beetles, no . . .

AFTERWORD

YOGI BERRA ONCE FAMOUSLY said: "It ain't over 'til the Fat Lady sings."

The Yankee catcher had a way with words that make a lot of sense. And I wish he could steer me to the "Fat Lady" because I am ready . . . way past ready . . . for the end of my health issues and treatments. At times it seems they are beginning to drag me down. I need a change of pace.

Without you realizing it---after mentioning Yogi---I have eased baseball into my medical manuscript. If you like baseball ---and most seniors like me feel the same way---we remember baseball as it used to be before steroids and tattoos and beards and such. We older fans remember "The Old Scotchman" Gordon McClendon, Roy Campanella, Mickey Mantle, Ted Williams, Warren Spahn, Whitey Ford, Johnny Mize, Reggie Jackson . . . the list could go on and on. But my greatest memory has nothing to do with any of those superstars.

Instead, I remember---at least most of it---the encounter between Ryne Duren and Jimmy Piersall because it provides us with a "life lesson." My memory is fading and I cannot remember exactly all of the pieces of that episode. In fact, some of what follows may not be factual, but all of it is fixed in my memory---factual or not. I have tried to research that encounter, but have had no luck. But, it provides a life lesson and here it goes . . . I believe you will enjoy reading it as much as I have recalled it and written it down:

* * *

A Life Lesson for Us All

Late September. Yankee Stadium. Yankees versus the Boston Red Sox. Score tied. Top of the ninth inning. Beantown runners are on first and second base. The multitude of Yankee fans are all standing. They are worried. The handful of Red Sox supporters are standing, wild with excitement and anticipation of what they hope will come. The Yankee manager has his head bowed, leaves the dugout, and slowly trudges to the pitcher's mound. Best I recall, it had to be Casey Stengel. He takes the ball from the harried Yankee hurler, turns toward the outfield, and waves his right hand. The Yankee fans know what's coming.

Ryne Duren is the best relief pitcher---not only for the Bronx Bombers---but in all of baseball. He is infamous for his wildness at times, but is equally acclaimed for his huge number of strikeouts. Duren has very poor vision, and his glasses are as thick as a Coke bottle. He trots across left field toward the infield and his favorite spot: the pitcher's mound at the historic stadium that "Ruth" built many years ago.

Jimmy Piersall, the zany, unpredictable but jovial and ego-filled centerfielder for the Sox, is the next-up batter. He stands erect in the on-deck circle, squeezing his Louisville Slugger bat. He watches Duren, who is now walking slowly to the mound.

Duren smooths over the holes in the dirt mound with his shoe, and prepares for his handful of warm-up pitches. His infielders gather around the mound---their very presence assures support. The Yankee fans sit down---they know what's coming. So do the Red Sox backers---they've seen it before.

Duren takes his position on the mound, facing third base so he can wheel around and throw to second base if the runner takes too big a lead off the base.

His first warm-up pitch dives into the ground about ten feet short of the plate. The ball careens past the Yankee catcher---it had to be Yogi---and dribbles up to the short wall in front of the grandstand. The ump tosses another ball to Duren. Piersall drops to one knee, using his bat for support. The second warm-up pitch is five feet right of the plate where a right-handed batter stands. Yogi leaps for the pitch, and the ball bounces off the end of his mitt. The noise from the fans turns to silence.

Duren catches another ball from the ump, rakes the mound with his shoe, and takes his stance, his right foot on the rubber. His third pitch sails six feet over Yogi's head and hits the protective screen in front of the first-row seats. Three warm-up pitches are enough for Duren. He walks a few steps toward second base and grabs the sticky bag that pitchers rely on. He is set to go. The noise begins again, and reaches an ear-shattering volume. Piersall is standing erect again, staring at Duren.

The ump says, "Play ball."

Piersall doesn't move, ignoring the ump's call. The ump takes a couple of steps out from behind the plate and waves to Piersall, and then points to the batter's box. Piersall turns toward the ump and nods his head from side to side---a clear "No." He assumes his normal batting stance, taps his bat on an imaginary plate, takes a practice swing---all of this happening while he is still in the on-deck circle. Dizzy Dean, the renowned broadcaster sitting alongside his sidekick Peewee Reese, loves it---reminds him of the old days. Some fans start to boo. Piersall nods sideways again.

Forgive me, but after all these intervening years, I can't recall how it ended. The entire scene was clear: Duren wanted to scare the hell out of Piersall and Piersall didn't want to be embarrassed. He wasn't afraid, he was petrified.

The life lesson is this: Duren was aggressive and wanted to get the upper hand. We seniors should be aggressive and need to get the upper hand as far as our health is concerned. Don't hold back---tell the doctor what's going on. Piersall was leery to face the music and what might happen. We need to get in the batter's box, face the music, and follow our doctor's orders. Get your health back, don't sit on the couch, staying at home, griping about your old age, and keep feeling bad. See your doctor and get well.

*   *   *

As I wind up this book, here are my thoughts with some advice for seniors thrown in:

- Now, almost three years since I found that lump on my neck, I feel fairly good. My cancer is in remission, my face looks as good as ever since the scars from the surgeries have nearly vanished, my tongue still has a small amount of feeling but I am working around that, my mouth is level, and I am determined to learn again how to chew and swallow. I need---and want---something better than Ensure to keep me healthy.
- I am anxious to avoid those waiting rooms, those narrow aisles, those crummy magazines, and dodging those Volkswagen beetles. Narrow aisles are not my favorite space.
- Tell your doctors and their staff that you appreciate their care and concern for you. Yes, that is their job, but they are genuinely concerned about your well-being. That is why they entered the medical field in the first place: they want to help others. Sure, you'll have to wait for a while in those waiting rooms before you get called into the exam room, but be patient and don't gripe about it—like I have.

*   *   *

"It Ain' Over 'Til . . ."

And, last but not least . . . whoa, wait a minute. Listen. What's that sound coming from the television? It can't be, but it is. On the TV screen, there stands a large middle-aged woman, wearing a long black dress with sequins sparkling from the stage lights, standing in front of a stationary microphone, in front of a big band, singing her heart out with clear, harmonious notes that you have heard from her over the years. Yes, it's Kate Smith.

Yogi would be so proud because it's finally over.
Adios.

ACKNOWLEDGEMENTS

A tip of my sombrero to the following friends, family, and publishing associates who have been helpful to me in putting together this book, or who have been very concerned and wired-in during the course of my various ailments. Thanks so much . . . you mean an awful lot to me, and I will be grateful for years to come:

Friends

- **Sonja and John Van Nortwick**. Regular phone calls and visits, checking on my progress. They have furnished me with a top-of-the-line walker, which I use much of the time, and a wheelchair, which I have not yet used, and hope I won't need to. Our monthly get-togethers with them, the Van Pelts (who follow) and Mary and I have been so much fun, and the wine and hors d'oeuvres have been great.
- **Sheryll and Don Van Pelt.** Wherever they've been . . . in El Paso or at their condo in Palm Springs . . . they've regularly checked on my well-being and anxious to chauffer us wherever we need to go. Don's golf stories, and tales of his impressionable years at Ohio State, always brighten our wine-and-snacks parties, and Sheryll's upbeat attitude and warm hospitality have been a godsend.
- **Reverend Ron Thomson.** When Rev. Bill Francis retired and moved to Central Texas, Reverend Ron inherited the regular chore of bringing communion to our house, and holding a brief but inspirational

communion service for Mary and me. Ron has never spoken or heard a single word that was not followed by one of his huge grins and a hug. You'll never have a negative attitude around Ron.

- **John Bauer.** With outstanding facilities at his business location, John took my several photographs, and converted them to meet printing requirements of iUniverse. He sized everyone, then forwarded them for placement in this book. John and I go back for many years, at one time business associates in the grocery business. Thanks, John, you did it again.

Family

- **Liliana and Joseph Welsh and children.** Not a day goes by without one of them checking on me. Joseph has accompanied Mary and me on many of my doctor appointments, and provides guidance and encouragement all the time, and Liliana has been right there to assist. When Patrick and Nathan are home from boarding school, they are at our house, taking care of our yard and anything else needed. Carling is our cookie-baker.
- **Jem Welsh.** Since Jem moved from California, he has been living with us while establishing his world-wide business in El Paso. He is a nutritionist, a body builder, and a meal-planner, and he constantly urges me to exercise and get back my strength. He helps Mary with some of the household chores, and is ready to accompany us to various medical visits.
- **Jean and Bill Manning**. Although they live hundreds of miles away on the Texas Gulf coast, we are constantly in their prayers. Bill is Mary's cousin, and more like an older brother. Bill is aware that a care-giver can get down-in-the-dumps, and he is on the phone at the right time to cheer Mary up.

- **Julie and Skip Gregory**. Whether they are at their home in Tallahassee, or on the road when Skip is speaking at conventions, we hear from them regularly---either by phone or by one of Julie's fantastic letters. Skip is Mary's little brother, and he assumes the "father" role when he suspects one of us needs his advice or assistance.

Publishing Associates

- **Mars Alma and Cherry Noel**. They have been my two primary contacts in dealing with iUniverse, my publisher. They have provided me with good advice, and steered me through their company's departments. Although the author has final say-so in some matters, they step in when necessary, putting their experience to work so that a good book emerges. Thanks to both.

ABOUT THE AUTHOR

JOHN F. WELSH JR. is a native of El Paso and resides there with his wife of over 40 years, Mary Louise. They recently sold their two West Texas supermarkets and are now---at long last ---fully retired. When John's health improves, he will be back on the golf course---and when John's health improves, Mary will be back doing what she wants to do instead of nursing John through his ailments. Mary is well qualified for the nursing chores because she is a licensed vocational nurse. She will soon be playing golf again, though it is likely---almost certain---she will <u>not</u> be playing with her husband.

John attended the University of Texas El Paso and the University of Missouri, studying journalism. He co-published a weekly newspaper in suburban El Paso, and worked as a news reporter for the El Paso Herald-Post for five years. He served during the Korean War, and then joined his family's grocery business in 1953. In 1966, he began a 17-year career in grocery wholesaling and distribution. John and Mary bought their first supermarket in 1983 and, over the following 32 years, operated up to five stores in West Texas.

John's writing background influenced him back to the computer in the early-2000s, and he authored an award-winning memoir about his and Mary's reuniting with John's Irish relatives after a gap of four generations. That book is entitled *Tipperary to Texas*.

They have four children: Dr. John F. Welsh III, a retired professor and dean of higher education at the University of Louisville, who lives with his wife Wendy in Kerrville, TX.; James William (Jem) Welsh, a certified nutritionist who has recently moved his world-wide practice from San Clemente,

CA. to El Paso, and who has two sons, Cody and Jameson, who reside with their families in San Antonio, TX; Jacquelyn Nell Welsh, a disabled Army veteran who lives in Las Vegas, NV; and Joseph Welsh, a former retail grocer who lives in El Paso with his wife, Liliana, and their three younger children, Patrick, Nathan, and Carling; two older children, Victoria and Johnathan, reside in Alpine, TX.

John and Mary's fourth son, David, passed away in August 2014.

Printed in the United States
By Bookmasters